BE COUNTED

Be Counted

WARREN W. WIERSBE

While this book is intended for
the reader's personal enjoyment
and profit, it is also designed for
group study. Study questions are
located at the end of the text.

Chariot Victor Publishing
A Division of Cook Communications

Chariot Victor Publishing,
A division of Cook Communications, Colorado Springs, Colorado 80918
Cook Communications, Paris, Ontario
Kingsway Communications, Eastbourne, England

Editor: Barbara Williams
Design: Bill Gray
Cover Photo: Image Bank
Study Questions: Susan Moroney

Library of Congress Cataloging-in-Publication Data

Wiersbe, Warren W.
     Be counted/by Warren W. Wiersbe.
       p. cm.
     ISBN 1-56476-703-5
     1. Bible. O.T. Numbers--Criticism, interpretation, etc.
I. Title.
BS1265.2.W54   1999   98-50299
222'.1406--dc21   CIP

3 4 5 6 7 8 9 10 Printing/Year 03 02

CONTENTS

To the memory of
GEORGE W. PATCHEN,
our beloved friend and accountant,
who knew how to count
and be counted.

PREFACE

In different parts of the world, the word "count" shows up with assorted meanings. "Count us out!" is what American teenagers say when they have their own plans for the day. ("Include us out" is a variation of this phrase.) To a fight fan, "counted out" means that the boxer is on his back in the ring and has lost the fight. "No count" is a brief way of saying that somebody isn't worth very much in the eyes of society.

To "count kin" is a Scottish term that means "to compare family trees" with somebody to see if the two of you might be distantly related. Thanks to modern science and science fiction, "countdown" is a very familiar word. It's the process of signaling the launching of a rocket by counting from a higher number (usually 10) down to zero. "Five, four, three, two, one, zero—*blast off!*"

But perhaps the most familiar use of the word "count" is as a synonym for dependability: "You can count on me!" It may have a military origin. Once soldiers are in position and have "counted off," they're ready to hear and obey their officer's orders. This is the way I'm using "count" in this book. To *Be Counted* means to be the kind of Christian God can depend on to get the job done right.

The Book of Numbers opens with a count of all the fighting men in the camp. They were *counted* but they couldn't be *counted on*, because all but two of them died during Israel's march through the wilderness. Then the new generation was counted, and they were people that the Lord could "count on." They trusted His Word, entered the Promised Land, and claimed it for their inheritance.

As never before, the church needs people on whom the Lord can depend. We have too much "cafeteria Christianity" these days, with God's people going from church to church, "sampling" ministry and not settling down to serve the Lord faithfully in the place where He's assigned them. No wonder we're losing so many battles.

Studying the Book of Numbers can help us better understand how God directs His people, why being faithful to Him is important, and how we can grow spiritually in the difficulties of life. We don't have to fail as did that first generation; we can be "more than conquerors through Him that loved us" (Rom. 8:37).

Warren W. Wiersbe

A Suggested Outline of the Book of Numbers

Key Theme: Man's failure and God's faithfulness
Key verses: Numbers14:8-9

I. At Sinai: Obeying the Lord (1:1–9:14)
1. Numbering the soldiers (1:1-54)
2. Organizing the tribes (2:1-34)
3. Assigning the duties (3–4)
4. Purifying the people (5–6)
5. Dedicating the tabernacle (7–8)
6. Celebrating the Passover (9:1-14)

II. To Kadesh: Tempting the Lord (9:15–12:16)
1. The camp marches (9:15–10:36)
2. The people complain (11:1-35)
3. Aaron and Miriam criticize Moses (12:1-16)

III. At Kadesh: Rebelling against the Lord (13–14)
1. Exploring the Promised Land (13:1-33)
2. Refusing to claim the land (14:1-9)
3. Turning away from the land (14:10-45)

IV. In the Wilderness: Learning from the Lord (15:1–20:13)
1. About sacrifices (15:1-31)
2. About authority (15:32–17:13)
3. About responsibility (18:1-32)
4. About purity (19:1-22)
5. About humility (20:1-29)

V. In Moab: A New Beginning from the Lord (20:14–36:13)
1. New victories (20:14-21; 21:1-35)
2. A new priest (20:22-29)
3. New dangers (22–25)
4. A new generation (26:1-65)
5. New regulations (27:1-11)
6. A new leader (27:12-23)
7. New commitment to the law (28–30)
8. New commitment to battle (31–32)
9. New laws for the new land (33–36)

ONE

Order in the Camp

The code name for the enterprise was "Operation Overlord." The more popular name was "D-Day"—June 6, 1943, when the combined Allied forces landed on "Omaha Beach" and signaled the beginning of the end of the war in Europe. It was the largest assembly of military personnel and materiel in the history of warfare. Historian Samuel Eliot Morison wrote, "The Allied forces of soldiers, sailors, aviators and supporting services amounted to 2.8 million men in England."[1]

Moses was about to launch his own "Operation Overlord," and his greatest desire was that Jehovah, the Lord of Hosts, truly be Lord over the whole enterprise. More than 2 million Jews were anticipating entering Canaan, conquering the inhabitants, claiming the land, and enjoying their promised inheritance. But before all of this could happen, Moses had to organize this assembly of former slaves who had been enjoying their freedom for only a year. It wasn't an easy task.

His preparation for conquest involved four stages: celebrating the Passover (9:1-14), numbering the soldiers (chap. 1), organizing the tribes (chap. 2), and assigning the priestly duties (chaps. 3–4).

1. Celebrating the Passover (Num. 9:1-14)

The events recorded in Num. 1–6 were preceded by those described in 7:1–9:15. We are now in the second year of Israel's national history (1:1; 9:1). The tabernacle was erected on the first day of the first month (Ex. 40:2, 17). The twelve tribal leaders began to bring their gifts on that day (Num. 7:1), a procedure that lasted twelve days (v. 78). On the thirteenth day, the Levites were consecrated (Num. 8), and on the fourteenth day, the Jews celebrated Passover (9:1-14).

The second Passover (Num. 9:1-5). It was only fitting that the Israelites began their second year of freedom by commemorating the awesome night when God delivered them from Egyptian bondage, "A night of solemn observance to the Lord" (Ex. 12:42, NKJV). In looking back, the people would appreciate what God had done for them, and they could teach their children the significance of Israel's "independence day" (Ex. 12:26-28; 13:8-16). Unless parents remind their children of what the Lord has done, it won't be long before the next generation will drift from the faith (Deut. 6:1-9; see 2 Tim. 2:2).

According to Exodus 12, each family had to slay a lamb, roast it, and eat it with unleavened bread and bitter herbs (see Num. 9:11). The bread contained no yeast for two reasons, one practical and the other symbolic. The practical reason was that the Jews had to be ready to leave Egypt at any time, so they couldn't wait for the dough to rise. The symbolic reason involves the fact that, to a Jew, leaven represents evil; and the Jews were to be a pure people. All yeast had to be removed from their houses before Passover and be kept out during the week that followed. (See 1 Cor. 5:1-8; Matt. 16:6, 12; Gal. 5:9.) The bitter herbs reminded the Jews of their cruel bondage when they were slaves in Egypt.

For Christians today, Passover speaks of Jesus Christ, the Lamb of God who died for the sins of the world (John 1:29; 1 Cor. 5:7; Isa. 53:7; 1 Peter 1:19; Rev. 5:6). Those who trust Him are redeemed from sin (1 Peter 1:18; Rom. 8:34; Eph. 1:7; Heb. 9:12) and may claim their spiritual inheritance in Christ (Eph. 1:3).

During the last Passover feast with His disciples, Jesus inaugurated what we call The Lord's Supper (Eucharist, Communion) to encourage His people to remember Him. This supper reminds us that Christ gave His body and shed His blood for our redemption (Matt. 26:26-30; Mark 14:22-25; Luke 22:17-20) and that He will one day come again to receive us (1 Cor. 11:23-34; 1 Thes. 4:13-18).

An emergency situation (Num. 9:6-12). Anyone who was defiled had to be put out of the camp, because defilement has a way of spreading (5:1-2). This meant that these men were forbidden to participate in Passover. This new situation demanded new wisdom, so Moses turned to the Lord for help (James 1:5). Since it was the Lord's Passover, only the Lord could change the rules.

God's reply was gracious: anyone who was defiled or absent from home during Passover the first month could celebrate the feast on the fourteenth day of the second month, but they had to be careful to follow the same divine instructions given in Exodus 12. God wasn't establishing a different Passover; He was only permitting His original Passover to be celebrated at a different time. None of the meat should be treated as common food ("leftovers"), and the lamb's bones must not be broken (see John 19:31-37).

Two warnings (Num. 9:13-14). This special consideration on the part of the Lord might lead some of the Israelites to start tampering with the divinely ordained Passover instructions, so God told Moses to warn them that the original rules were still in force, both for the first month and the second. Any Jews who were qualified to celebrate Passover the first month but didn't do so, hoping to do it more conveniently the second month, would be disciplined by God. What is meant by "cut off" isn't explained here; it might mean exclusion from the camp, or it could mean death. Just as Passover was a serious matter to the Jews, so the Lord's Supper must be taken seriously by Christians (1 Cor. 11:28-30).

The second warning had to do with resident aliens in the

camp, people who were not born under the Abrahamic Covenant and had not received the sign of circumcision. They might think that the second-month Passover was not as restricted as the first-month observance, but they would be wrong. Gentiles would have to become Jewish proselytes if they wanted to observe Passover with the Jews (Ex. 12:19, 43).

A *great tragedy*. This was the last Passover the Jews celebrated until Joshua led them into the Promised Land years nearly forty years later (Josh. 5:10). Because of their unbelief and rebellion at Kadesh-Barnea (Num. 13–14), the people twenty years and older were rejected by the Lord and died during Israel's wilderness march. When Joshua led the new generation into Canaan, the males received the sign of the covenant and God restored His people into His good favor (Josh. 5:2-9). It was a new beginning for Israel in their new land.

2. Numbering the soldiers (Num. 1:1-54)

The second month of the second year, thirteen months after the Exodus, Israel had to start preparing for battle. If Genesis is the book of beginnings and Exodus the book of redemption, then Numbers is the book of warfare. The Jews were in enemy territory, marching toward the land God would help them conquer, and they had to organize for confrontation and conflict. The phrase "able to go forth to war" is used fourteen times in this chapter. If God were to number the believers in the church today according to their ability to wage spiritual warfare, we wonder how big the army would be.

The order given (Num. 1:1-3). Over 150 times in the Book of Numbers, it's recorded that God spoke to Moses and gave him instructions to share with the people. In fact, Numbers opens with God speaking to His servant, and it closes with a reminder that God had spoken to Israel through Moses (36:13). One of the Hebrew names for this book is "And He spoke," taken from Numbers 1:1.[2] Apart from the revelation of God's will, Israel would not have known what to do or where to camp. "You led Your people like a flock by the hand of Moses and Aaron" (Ps.

77:20, NKJV).

God's command was that Moses, Aaron, and the tribal leaders take a census of the men who were available to serve in the army. Israel's army wasn't made up of volunteers, for each able-bodied man, twenty years of age or older, was expected to take his place and serve the Lord and the people.[3]

Some people are disturbed by the emphasis on warfare in certain parts of the Bible, and a few denominations have even removed from their hymnals militant songs like "Onward, Christian Soldiers." But their fears and criticisms are unfounded. "The Lord is a man of war" (Ex. 15:3) when it comes to punishing sin and removing evil. The nations that Israel destroyed in Canaan were living in abominable moral filth and sinning against a flood of light, and the Lord had been long-suffering with them (Gen. 15:13-16; Rom. 1:18ff). Would anybody today criticize a surgeon for removing a cancerous life-threatening tumor from a patient's body? Yet that's what God did for society when He used Israel to judge the degenerate nations in Canaan.

Furthermore, the military image is used frequently in the New Testament, even by Jesus (Matt. 16:18) and especially by Paul (Rom. 8:31; Eph. 6:10-18; 2 Cor. 10:3-5; 1 Cor. 9:7; 2 Tim. 2:1-4). The Christian life is a battleground, not a playground, and there's an enemy to fight and territory to gain for the Lord. God declared war on Satan long ago (Gen. 3:15) and there can be no neutrality in this spiritual conflict, for Jesus said, "He that is not with Me is against Me" (Matt. 12:30).

The leaders appointed (Num. 1:4-16). Moses and Aaron were assisted in the census by the appointed leader of each tribe. These tribal leaders are also named in chapters 2; 7; and 10. It wasn't difficult to make the count because the nation was organized by households, families (clans), and tribes (Josh. 7:14), and there were rulers for each unit of ten, one hundred, and one thousand Israelites (Ex. 18:21). Note that Nahshon (Num. 1:7) was in the family tree of David (Ruth 4:20-22) and therefore an ancestor of Christ (Matt. 1:4). Note also that each person had to prove his lineage (Num. 1:18) so that no unqualified outsider entered the army of the Lord.

The numbers recorded (Num. 1:17-26). The numbers are rounded off to the nearest hundred, except the report from Gad, which is rounded off to fifty (vv. 24-25). The total number of warriors from age twenty and upward was 603,550 (v. 46). Except for Joshua and Caleb, all these men died during Israel's years of wandering in the wilderness. The second census totaled 601,730 men (26:51), an army that entered the land and claimed the inheritance.

The Levites exempted (Num. 1:47-54). The three sons of Levi were Gershon, Kohath, and Merari (Gen. 46:11); Moses and Aaron were descendants of Kohath (Num. 3:14-24) and Aaron was the first high priest. Only the sons of Aaron were allowed to minister at the altar (vv. 1-4) and the Levites assisted the priests in their ministry. Supervised by the high priest, the Levites dismantled the tabernacle when the camp relocated, carried the various tabernacle parts, furnishings, and vessels during the march, and then erected the tabernacle at the new location.

The Levites camped around the tabernacle, which stood in the center of the camp, with Kohath on the south, Merari on the north, and Gershon on the west. Moses and Aaron camped on the east, at the gate of the tabernacle. In this way, the Levites protected the tabernacle from intruders and, being next to the tabernacle, would see when the cloud signaled that the camp was going to move.

Because of their important ministry as assistants to the priests, the Levites were exempted from military duty. The tabernacle was the most important structure in the entire camp, and only the priests and Levites could attend to it. Therefore, they weren't counted in the military census. Worship and warfare may seem unrelated, but in God's economy, they go together. One of the major themes of the Book of Revelation is God's warfare against evil on earth and His receiving worship in heaven. Unless the people of God are right with the Lord in their worship, they can't face their enemies and defeat them in warfare. "Let the high praises of God be in their mouth, and a two-edged sword in their hand" (Ps. 149:6).

3. Organizing the tribes (Num. 2:1-34)

When the motions of the pillar of cloud over the tabernacle announced that the camp would move, it would have been difficult if not impossible to break camp and start the march quickly and efficiently without some kind of order in the camp. "Let all things be done decently and in order" (1 Cor. 14:40) is an admonition for God's people in every age, "for God is not the author of confusion" (v. 33).

We've already seen that Moses and Aaron, with the priests and Levites, camped immediately around the tabernacle. Each of the twelve tribes was assigned a specific place to camp, also with reference to the tabernacle; for God dwelt at the heart of the camp, and each tribe's location was determined by the Lord.

Judah, Issachar, and Zebulun, all descendants of Leah, camped to the east, with a total of 186,400 men. Since the entrance to the tabernacle was there, it was important to have the largest number of soldiers protecting it. Reuben, Simeon, and Gad camped south of the tabernacle with 151,450 men. Ephraim and Manasseh, the descendants of Joseph, encamped west of the tabernacle, along with Benjamin, a total of 108,100 men. Thus, all the descendants of Rachel camped together. On the north side of the tabernacle were Dan, Asher, and Naphtali, with 157,600 men.

Whenever the camp moved, the ark of the covenant went before, carried by the priests. Then the tribes of Judah, Issachar, and Zebulun marched next, followed by the Gershonites and Merarites carrying the tabernacle proper (frames, curtains, coverings). Next came Reuben, Simeon, and Gad, followed by the Kohathites carrying the tabernacle furnishings. Ephraim, Manasseh, and Benjamin were next, while Dan, Asher, and Naphtali brought up the rear. The largest number of soldiers (186,400) led the way and the next largest (157,600) were the rear guard.

The twelve tribes had to be careful not to camp too close to the tabernacle, for that area was reserved for the priests and

15

Levites (Num. 2:2). To venture too near to the sacred tent could mean death (1:51). Also, each tribe was to display its standard and each family its banner (v. 52; 2:2). Nowhere in Scripture are we told the colors of these tribal banners or the emblems that were on them, and it's useless to conjecture. Jewish tradition suggests that the colors were those of the twelve gems in the high priest's breastplate (Ex. 28:15-29), but we can't be certain what some of those colors were. Jewish tradition also states that four of the tribal emblems came from Ezekiel 1:10 (and see Rev. 4:7) and assigned the lion to Judah (Gen. 49:9), the ox to Ephraim, the man to Reuben, and the eagle to Dan. But this is nowhere affirmed in Scripture.

With the pillar of cloud hovering over the center of the camp by day and ablaze with fire at night, and the tents of the various tribes arranged in their assigned places, the camp of Israel must have been an awesome sight. When the Prophet Balaam looked at the camp from the mountain heights, he said, "How beautiful are your tents, O Jacob, your dwelling places, O Israel! Like valleys they spread out, like gardens beside a river, like aloes planted by the Lord, like cedars beside the waters" (Num. 24:5-6, NIV).

In God's plan, Israel and the church are two different peoples (1 Cor. 10:32), but you can't help but see Israel's camp as an illustration of what God's church ought to be in this world: a pilgrim people following the Lord, with His glory at the heart of everything and His presence leading the way. Israel was one people, united in the Lord and to each other. Yet each separate company was recognized by God, displayed its own unique banner, occupied its own special place, and marched at the Lord's command.

4. Assigning the duties (Num. 3:1–4:49)

These two chapters are devoted to the Levites, the men who served the Lord by assisting the priests in their ministry at the tabernacle. Moses records two numberings of the Levites, those one month old and older and those twenty years old and older, as well as the duties assigned to them. The Levites had no inheritance in the Promised Land but lived from a tithe of the gifts that the people brought to the Lord (18:20-24).

The priests (Num. 3:1-4). The priests were the descendants of Aaron, the first high priest, who had four sons: Nadab, Abihu, Eleazar, and Ithamar (Ex. 6:23). Nadab and Abihu brought unauthorized worship into the sanctuary and were killed by the Lord (Lev. 10).[4] Eleazar was chief over the Levites (Num. 3:32) and eventually replaced his father as high priest (20:22-29). Ithamar had received the offerings for the building of the tabernacle (Ex. 38:21) and was in charge of the Gershonites and Merarites (Num. 4:28, 33). It was no insignificant thing to be one of God's priests, for the priests were God's anointed servants, especially consecrated for His glory (Ex. 28–29).

The gift of the Levites (Num. 3:5-1). God looked on Israel as His firstborn son (Ex. 4:22). He had spared Israel's firstborn at Passover but had slain the firstborn sons of Egypt (11:1-7; 12:29-30). For this reason, every firstborn male in Israel, whether human or animal, belonged to the Lord and had to be redeemed by a sacrifice (13:1-2, 11-13; 22:29-30; 34:19-20; Luke 2:7, 22-23).

The entire nation of Israel was to be a "kingdom of priests" before God (Ex. 19:5-6), and He appointed a special priesthood to help His people obey His law and bear witness of His goodness. The Levites were God's gift to the priests, substitutes for the redeemed firstborn sons of Israel who already belonged to God. The Levites did for the Lord and the priests the service that the firstborn sons would have done, for the Levites ministered in their place.

The levitical census and duties (Num. 3:14–4:49). Two different censuses were taken of the Levites. Moses first counted every male, one month old and older, to make sure there were enough Levites to substitute for all the firstborn in Israel. There were 7,500 Gershonites (3:22), 8,600 Kohathites (v. 28), and 6,200 Merarites (vv. 33-34), a total of 22,000 Levites.[5] When Moses numbered the firstborn males in Israel, he found 22,273 (vv. 40-43), so the extra 273 men had no Levites to represent them in the sanctuary. These 273 males were redeemed by paying five shekels each, and the money was given to Aaron to be used for the service of the tabernacle.

The second census was of all the Levites, ages thirty to fifty, who were able to serve in the sanctuary (4:1-3, 21-23, 29-30); and the total was 8,580 (vv. 46-49). According to 8:24, the Levites began to serve at age twenty-five, so it's likely that the younger men went through a five-year training period to prepare them for their work. They had a great deal to learn about the sacrifices and the tabernacle service, and it was dangerous to make mistakes. Later, David lowered the starting age to twenty (1 Chron. 23:24-25).

The Gershonites (3:21-26; 4:21-28, 38-41) were numbered at 7,500, with 2,630 old enough to serve (4:40). They camped at the west end of the tabernacle, and had Eliasaph as their leader. Their responsibility was to transport the coverings, hangings, and framework of the tabernacle, and all the equipment that pertained to them; for this work they were given two carts and four oxen (7:7). Ithamar the priest supervised their work.

The Kohathites (3:27-32; 4:1-20, 34-37) numbered 8,600 men, of whom 2,750 were old enough to serve (4:36). They camped on the south side of the tabernacle and had Elizaphan as their leader. They were responsible for carrying the furniture in the sanctuary, and 4:1-20 explains the procedure. When the camp was about to move, Aaron and his sons would enter the holy place, take down the veil, and use it to cover the ark of the covenant. They would put over this a protective covering of skins and then a cloth of blue. They then put the wooden staves into the rings on the ark so that four of the men could carry it before the marching nation.

Once the ark was safely covered, the other pieces of furniture were covered in a similar manner. First they covered the table of showbread, then the lampstand and the golden altar of incense, and finally the altar of burnt offering. The various vessels and implements pertaining to each piece of furniture were also packed. Each of these sacred items was fitted for staves and the Kohathites carried the pieces of furniture on their shoulders.[6] It was important that the furnishings be covered lest some inquisitive Levite look at them and incur the judgment of God (vv. 16-20). Aaron's son Eleazar was in charge of the work of the Kohathites (3:32), and it was also his task to carry the oil for the lampstand, the incense for the golden altar, the flour for the daily meal offering, and the holy anointing oil (4:16).

The Gershonites and Merarites had wagons for carrying their burdens, but the Kohathites had none (7:1-9). The sacred furniture of the tabernacle had to be borne on the shoulders of the sanctified servants of God. When David had the ark brought into Jerusalem, he didn't obey this rule, and it led to the death of Uzzah (2 Sam. 6). The Kohathites were burden-bearers, but their burdens were precious, very important to the people, and appointed by the Lord. Certainly they considered it a privilege to carry the sacred furnishings of the sanctuary on their shoulders through the wilderness.

The Merarites (Num. 3:33-37; 4:29-33, 42-45) numbered 6,200, of whom 3,200 were the proper age to serve (v. 44). They camped to the north of the tabernacle and had Zuriel as their leader. They had an especially difficult task because they carried the heavy boards of the tabernacle, as well as the bars, pillars, and silver sockets into which the pillars fit. No wonder Moses gave them four wagons and eight oxen to help them with their work (7:8). Aaron's son Ithamar supervised their ministry.

All this information about the ministry of the Levites reminds us that our God is concerned with details and wants His work to be done by the people He has chosen and in the way He has appointed. Nothing in the camp of Israel was left to chance or human contrivance. Each Levite and priest knew his responsibilities and was expected to "serve God with reverence and godly fear" (Heb. 12:28). Caring for the tabernacle was serious work, a matter of life and death.

The chapters also remind us that not everybody has the same burdens to bear. The Gershonites and Merarites could put their burdens on wagons, but the Kohathites had to carry their burdens on their shoulders. There are some burdens we can share (Gal. 6:2), but there are other burdens that only we can bear (v. 5).[7]

Finally, we must note that our God believes in organization, but the organization is a means to an end and not an end in itself. One of my coworkers at Moody Church liked to say, "Remember, the church is an organism, not an organization." But I would remind him that if an organism isn't organized, it will die! Yes, the church is a living spiritual organism, but it's also an organization. If an army isn't organized, it can't fight the enemy successfully; if a family isn't organized, it will experience nothing but chaos and confusion.

God was preparing His people to engage enemy nations and defeat them. It was important that the camp be orderly and the work of the tabernacle be organized. Otherwise, the worship would not please God and the warfare would lead to defeat.

We live in an age not unlike that described in the Book of Judges, when "every man did that which was right in his own eyes" (Jud. 17:6; 18:1; 19:1; 21:25). But God's word to His people is just the opposite: "See that you make all things according to the pattern shown you on the mountain" (Heb. 8:5, NKJV; see Ex. 25:40).

When God's work is done God's way, in obedience to God's truth, it will never lack God's blessing.

TWO

Dedication and Celebration—Part I

When Mohandas K. Gandhi was the spiritual leader of India, a missionary asked him what he thought was the biggest obstacle to Christian missions in India, and Gandhi replied, "Christians."

We may not like his answer, but we do have to face the fact that too often God's people get in the way of God's work. This is no better illustrated than in the Book of Numbers where we see Israel repeatedly disobeying God and suffering for it. This explains why the Lord laid down some plain and practical rules for daily life in the camp of Israel. Israel was God's chosen people, separated from the other nations, and God wanted them to be different in the way they lived. What kind of people did the Lord want them to be?

1. A clean people (Num. 5:1-31)

God's glorious presence dwelt in the camp of Israel (5:3; Ex. 29:45) and therefore the camp had to be pure and holy in His sight. "I will walk among you and be your God, and you shall be My people," was His promise (Lev. 26:12, NKJV), and with that gracious promise came the solemn responsibility: "You shall be holy, for I am holy" (Lev. 11:44-45).[1]

The concepts of "clean" and "unclean" were vital to daily life in Israel. Cleanliness involved much more than personal hygiene; it involved being acceptable to God in what they ate, what they wore, and how they conducted themselves at home and in public. The Israelites were in the infancy of their faith, and God used familiar pictures to teach them spiritual truth. He compared sin to disease and defilement and holiness to health and cleanliness (Lev. 11–15). Unclean people were put out of the camp until they had met the ceremonial requirements for reentry.

The word "defiled" is used nine times in Numbers 5, and three kinds of defilement are described.

Physical defilement (Num. 5:1-4). Scholars aren't agreed on what leprosy was in ancient days, and some modern translations prefer "infectious skin disease." Whatever it was, leprosy was a dreaded disease that made the victims ceremonially unclean. They had to live outside the camp, and if anybody approached them, they had to cry out, "Unclean, unclean!" (See Lev. 13.) If they were cured, they had to go through a lengthy process of cleansing before being admitted back into the camp (Lev. 14).

The second defiled group was made up of people from whose bodies fluid was being discharged (see Lev. 15). The discharge might be natural (vv. 16-18, 25-30) or unnatural (vv. 1-15, 19-24), but it still made the people unclean. Some of these discharges might be caused by venereal diseases or other infections which would make the people toxic, so isolating them helped to maintain the health of the camp.

The third group was composed of people who had touched a dead body, whether human or animal. The law concerning defilement by the dead is spelled out in Numbers 19:11-22 and Leviticus 21:1-4. The decayed carcass of an animal was likely to be contaminated and therefore able to spread disease, but even human corpses were considered unclean. Those who prepared their loved ones for burial were ceremonially unclean for a week and had to go through ritual cleansing before being received back into the camp.

Although health and hygiene were involved in these laws, their basic purpose was to teach the Jews the meaning of separation and holiness. Israel was to be a clean people and this was accomplished by obeying God's Word in every area of life. God's people today need to take this to heart: "Let us cleanse ourselves from all filthiness of the flesh and spirit, perfecting holiness in the fear of God" (2 Cor. 7:1).

When our Lord ministered on earth, He ignored the laws of uncleanness and touched lepers (Luke 5:12-15), people with issues touched Him (8:43-48), and He even touched the dead (7:11-17; 8:49-56). The touch of the Great Physician brought healing to the victims but didn't defile the Son of God. It was only when He died on the cross that He bore our defilement and the awful "disease" of our sin (1 Peter 2:24; Isa. 53:4-6).

Interpersonal defilement (Num. 5: 5-10). The person who committed a trespass against another had to confess it and make restitution. (See Lev. 6:1-7; 7:1-10.) It wasn't enough just to confess the sin, say, "I'm sorry," and then bring a trespass offering to the priest. The offender had to pay the injured party (or a relative, or the priest) an amount of money equivalent to the loss incurred and add to it another 20 percent. In this way, the Lord taught His people that sin is costly and hurts people, and that true repentance demands honest restitution.

But another factor was involved. Israel was about to confront their enemies, and there could be no unity in the army if the people were in conflict with one another because of unresolved offenses. The soldiers would be alienated from each other and from the Lord, and that could lead to defeat. True unity begins with everybody being right with God and with each other.

Marital defilement (Num. 5:11-31). Faithfulness in marriage is a foundation stone for every society, for as goes the home, so goes the nation. In Israel, adultery not only defiled the people involved but also the land itself, and it was a sin detestable to God (Lev. 18:20, 24-29). Adultery was a capital offense. If proved guilty, both the adulterer and the adulteress were stoned to death (Deut. 22:22-24).

Suppose a husband suspected that his wife had been unfaithful to him but he didn't have witnesses to prove it? What could he do? If his suspicions were wrong, the longer his feelings smoldered, the more damage they would do to him, his wife, and their family. If his suspicions were correct, would her sin introduce spurious issue—or even disease—into his family? To help solve this dilemma, the Lord instituted this test.

Let's look at the procedure first and then consider the issues that are involved in the test.[2]

First, the husband brought his wife to the priest at the door of the tabernacle, along with the prescribed offering (Num. 5:15-16). This test was a public event that others could see and hear. There the priest presented her to the Lord, because God alone was the Judge in this case (vv. 15-16; Lev. 5:1-13). The phrase, "before the Lord," is found four times in this passage (Num. 5:16, 18, 25, 30), and the name of the Lord is mentioned twice in the oath (v. 21). The offering was the humblest possible gift, the kind a poor person would bring, and it was presented without oil and frankincense. The couple stood before the Lord as the poorest of the poor.

Second, the priest took water from the laver and dust from the tabernacle floor and mixed them in a clay vessel (v. 17). Perhaps the dust was a reminder of man's humble origin (Gen. 2:7) as well as his ultimate destiny—death (Ps. 22:15). Third, the priest loosened the woman's hair, letting the tresses fall as if she were in mourning (Num. 5:18). A woman's hair is her glory and covering, and in this act, she was presenting her glory to the Lord and hiding nothing from Him (1 Cor. 11:15). At the same time, the priest put the offering into her hands.

Fourth, the priest put the wife under oath before God (Num. 5:19) and then announced the curses attached to the oath (vv. 20-22). She submitted to God's righteous judgment by saying, "Amen, amen," which means, "Let it be so." Fifth, the priest then wrote the curses on a scroll and washed them off into the bitter water (v. 23). Sixth, the woman then drank the water (v. 24).

The word "bitter," used five times in the passage (vv. 18-19, 23-24), doesn't refer to the taste of the water but the effects in her body. If she was guilty, God would send her bitter suffering.

Seventh, as the woman drank the water, the priest took the offering from her hands and presented it to the Lord. If the woman was indeed guilty, the results would prove it. If she conceived, the baby would miscarry; or she would become barren for the rest of her life. She would feel in her body the terrible consequences of her sins and live with those consequences until the day of her death. Of course, for a Jewish wife to be childless was a tragedy, for her most important task in life was to give her husband heirs and maintain his name in Israel (Gen. 30:1-2; Ruth 4:14).[3]

Now let's consider some of the issues involved in this ceremony. There's no record in Scripture that any husband ever used it or that any accused wife asked for it. Perhaps the very existence of this law proved a barrier to adultery and a warning that sin would be found out. There are clearly some built-in "roadblocks" that would make a husband hesitate to rush to the priest and ask for his wife to be tried.

To begin with, it was a public event, performed at the door of the tabernacle, and the whole camp could know about it. Would a husband want to expose his marital problems that openly, especially when he couldn't know the results of the trial?[4]

Furthermore, what transpired there told something about the husband as well as about the wife. If the husband loved his wife and was deeply hurt by her possible infidelity, why would he want to expose her publicly? But if he didn't love her and only wanted to hurt her, he might be embarrassed and proved wrong. A wise man would think twice before having his wife judged this way.

The husband would have to live with the consequences. If his suspicions were proved wrong, he owed his wife an apology and had to work at rebuilding the relationship. (Why wasn't he punished in some way for false accusation?) If she was found guilty, he had to live with her, wonder who her lover was, and suffer with the physical consequences of the curse and her bad reputation. She could never bear him children, but he still had to provide for her and for any children she gave him before committing her sin.

There are many perplexing questions associated with this ritual, but let's not miss the major message: God wants purity in marriage, and husbands and wives can't escape the bitter consequences of marital unfaithfulness. God can forgive adultery (John 8:1-11) and husbands and wives can make new beginnings in the Lord. However, adultery hurts everybody, and it's sometimes difficult to live with the consequences of forgiven sin.

2. A separated people (Num. 6:1-21)

Don't confuse "Nazirite" with "Nazarene." Jesus was called a "Nazarene" because He came from Nazareth, a city despised by the people of Judea (John 1:43-46).[5] The word "Nazirite" comes from a Hebrew word that means "to set apart, to dedicate." Jesus was not a Nazirite because He touched dead bodies and drank the fruit of the vine, both of which were forbidden to Nazirites.

Separation described (Num. 6:1-8). Nazirites were Jewish men or women who dedicated themselves wholly to the Lord to fulfill the Nazirite vow of total separation. (In the KJV, the words "separate" and "separation" are used sixteen times in this chapter.) The Nazirite vow had both positive and negative aspects: positively, it means being devoted to God; negatively, it meant abstaining from things God did not allow. Each Nazirite had a different goal in mind, but all of them wanted to glorify the Lord and obey His Word. They didn't isolate themselves from society but rather were witnesses to others of the importance of total devotion to the Lord. Their vow was for a specified period (Acts 21:23-27) and a specified purpose.

Three responsibilities were involved in the Nazirite vow. First, they were not to drink wine, grape juice, vinegar, or fermented drinks, nor were they allowed to eat grapes, raisins, or even the skins and seeds of grapes! Second, they had to let their hair grow as a sign they were devoted especially to God. Since female

Nazirites would already have long hair, perhaps they left it loose and somewhat unkempt as a mark of their dedication. Third, they were never to touch a corpse, even that of a close relative.

Separation defiled (Num. 6:9-12). Nobody but God can control the circumstances of life, and a Nazirite might accidentally be defiled. If that happened, he had to wait a week and on the seventh day shave his head. Since the period of dedication was suddenly over, and the hair was the sign of that dedication, the defiled hair had to go. However, the shorn hair wasn't made a part of the sacrifice as with the Nazirites who had completed their vows (v. 18).

On the eighth day, the former Nazirite met the priest at the brazen altar and offered the required sacrifices: a bird for a sin offering, a second bird for a burnt offering, and a lamb for a trespass offering. This enabled the person to rededicate himself or herself to the Lord and make a new beginning. It was another opportunity to fulfill the vow made to the Lord. Believers today need to realize that no failure need be permanent. Presbyterian pastor Alexander Whyte (1837–1921) said, "The victorious Christian life is a series of new beginnings."

Separation fulfilled (Num. 6:13-21). Nazirites who successfully completed their period of dedication came with their sacrifices to the priest and he offered them to the Lord.[6] First the priest sacrificed a year-old ewe lamb for a sin offering, for the Nazirites' period of dedication didn't make them sinless. Then the priest offered a year-old male lamb as a burnt offering, which symbolized total dedication to the Lord. Along with the basket of unleavened bread, he then offered a ram for the peace offering (fellowship offering), plus the meal offering and the drink offering. The bread and the peace offering would later become part of a fellowship meal at the tabernacle which the worshiper could share with others. According to the levitical law, the priest got his share of the offerings, for this was how he was supported.

One of the most important parts of the ceremony was the shaving of the Nazirite's head and the placing of the hair on the altar fire under the peace offering. It was a special offering to the

Lord because the long hair symbolized the vow the Nazirite had made to the Lord and had successfully fulfilled. Once these instructions had been obeyed, the Nazirite was allowed to drink wine.[7]

Nobody is saved by making and keeping a vow. Salvation is the gift of God to those who believe, not a reward to those who behave. However, there are some people who are led of the Lord to make special vows to God, not to get something from Him but to give something to Him, and as long as these vows don't contradict Scripture, they can be blessed of God (Pss. 22:25; 50:14; 61:5, 8; 76:11; 116:14). People will make vows to God just so He'll get them out of trouble (Ps. 66:14; Jonah 2:9), and some of these people will forget their promises when they're safe and comfortable again. But it's a dangerous thing to make promises to God and not keep them (Ecc. 5:1-7).

3. A blessed people (Num. 6:22-27)

The priests were given the privilege of serving at the altar and ministering in the sanctuary, but they were also allowed to bless God's people in the name of the Lord. We use this blessing today, for it belongs to us as well as to Israel. The church has been blessed with "every spiritual blessing" through the Lord Jesus Christ (Eph. 1:3) and we can claim this benediction through Him.

If ever a nation was blessed, it was the nation of Israel. God called them in His grace, rescued them from bondage, gave them His holy Word, gave them the Promised Land, and dwelt with them in the sanctuary; and He gave these blessings to no other nation. Of course, the greatest blessing of all was the sending of His Son through the nation of Israel, for "salvation is of the Jews" (John 4:22; see Rom. 9:1-5).

The threefold use of the name of the Lord suggests that our God is a Trinity of persons: God the Father, God the Son, and God the Holy Spirit. The Father is the Lord (Ps. 110:1), and so is the Son (Rom. 10:9), and so is the Spirit (2 Cor. 3:17). You see the Trinity in Matthew 3:16-17; 28:19-20; John 3:34-35; and

2 Corinthians 13:14, as well as many other places in the Bible. Ephesians 1:3-14 is actually a hymn to the Trinity: Father (vv. 3-6), Son (vv. 7-12), and Spirit (vv. 13-14).

The pronouns in this benediction are singular, meaning that God's blessings come to us personally; but there is a plural pronoun in Numbers 6:27, "I will bless them." God blesses the nation by blessing individuals, and by blessing the nation, He blesses the world. God promised Abraham, "I will bless you . . . and you will be a blessing" (Gen. 12:2, NIV). We bless the world by sharing God's truth, often one person at a time.

We need the blessings that God lists here: to be cared for by the Lord who watches over us; to have the smile of His face upon us and the riches of His grace given to us; to have Him pay attention to us when we call; and, as the result of these things, to enjoy His peace in our hearts. Peace (shalom) is one of the great words in the Hebrew vocabulary, and it means much more than the absence of storm and trouble around us. It involves quietness of heart within us, spiritual health and spiritual prosperity, adequacy for the demands of life, and the kind of spiritual well-being that rises above circumstances. George Morrison defined "peace" as "the possession of adequate resources," which is what Paul had in mind when he wrote Philippians 4:6-20.

4. A generous people (Num. 7:1-89)

On the first day of the first month, in the second year after Israel was delivered from Egypt, the tabernacle was erected and dedicated to the Lord (Ex. 40). On that day the twelve tribes of Israel began to bring special offerings to the Lord to be used by the priests and Levites in the tabernacle service. The people had donated generously to the building of the tabernacle (Ex. 25:1-8; 35:4–36:7), and now they were contributing to its ministry and maintenance.

A cursory reading of this long chapter (the longest in the Pentateuch) might give the impression that it contains nothing but repetition, for on twelve successive days each of the tribal leaders brought identical gifts. But we must not miss the point that God took notice of each gift, each leader, and each tribe on each successive day. In fact, each leader is mentioned twice, at the beginning of the report and at the end. We met these leaders in Numbers 1:5-16 and 2:3-32. The order is the same as that established for Israel whenever they marched to a new location.

While it's impossible by modern prices to calculate the value of these gifts, it's obvious that this was a very costly and generous offering. No doubt the twelve leaders got together and decided what to give, and then they gave their respective tribes opportunity to contribute. The gifts were both expensive and useful, showing generosity and practicality. The silver plates and bowls, and the gold dish (spoon, KJV), were needed for the priests' ministry in the tabernacle, as were their contents of flour and incense. Of course, the twenty-one animals for sacrifices that each leader brought would represent a considerable amount of money, a total of 252 beasts!

The fact that God noted and recorded each name and each gift indicates His love for and interest in the individual believer. He knows our names (John 10:3) and has recorded them individually in His heavenly register (Luke 10:20; Phil. 4:3). When we stand before the Lord, He will see us individually, "and then shall every man have praise of God" (1 Cor. 4:5) and "every man shall receive his own reward according to his own labor" (3:8). Nobody will be overlooked and nobody will be lost in the crowd.

David kept a register of the names of his "mighty men" (2 Sam. 23:8-39), and Paul sent greetings and appreciation to his friends in Rome (Rom. 16), twenty-six of whom he named specifically and two that he simply mentioned. David was a great warrior, but where would he have been without his mighty men? Paul was a great apostle and evangelist, but he needed his helpers to get the job done.

Just as with His ancient people, God wants His people today to be clean and separated, "unspotted from the world" (James 1:27). Campbell Morgan said that when the church was the least like the world, the church did the most for the world. We are a people blessed of the Lord, and with these blessings comes the obligation to be a blessing to others. God wants us to be a generous people, supporting the local church and helping the work of the Lord around the world as He directs us.

Can God count on us?

THREE

Dedication and Celebration—Part II

We are still examining the events that occurred in the camp of Israel at Mount Sinai on the day the tabernacle was erected and dedicated to God (7:1; Ex. 40:2, 17). It was the first day of the first month of the second year after Israel's exodus from Egypt.

Everything that was done in the camp of Israel was ordered by the Lord. In the holy place of the tabernacle, before the veil, Moses would speak to God and God would speak to Moses from the mercy seat (Num. 7:89). Then Moses would pass along God's orders to the people of Israel. "So the Lord spoke to Moses face to face, as a man speaks to his friend" (Ex. 33:11, NKJV).

Two things are involved here: divine revelation and divinely chosen leadership. All of God's people comprise a holy priesthood (Ex. 19:6; 1 Peter 2:5, 9)[1], but the Lord has given spiritual leaders to His people (Eph. 4:11-16) and these leaders should be respected and obeyed (Num. 12:6-8; Heb. 13:7-9, 17). In the church today, God doesn't speak audibly to His people as He did to Moses; but as God's people worship together, pray, and study

---

* We have already covered 9:1-14 in chapter 1.

His Word, He reveals His will. "Prove all things; hold fast that which is good" (1 Thes. 5:21). God spoke to Moses about three important matters: caring for the lamps (Num. 8:1-4), dedicating the Levites (vv. 5-26), and obeying His guidance as the nation marched to Canaan (9:15–10:10).

1. Caring for the lamps (Num. 8:1-4)

The tabernacle was divided into two parts: the holy of holies where God's glory rested above the mercy seat on the ark, and the holy place which was separated from the holy of holies by the veil. There were three pieces of furniture in the holy place: the table for the twelve loaves of bread, the golden altar of incense before the veil, and the golden lampstand with its seven lamps.[2]

When the tabernacle was dedicated to the Lord, God's glory moved in (Ex. 40:34-35) and God's fire consumed the sacrifices on the altar (Lev. 9:23-24). But God didn't light the seven lamps on the golden lampstand in the holy place. This was the obligation of Aaron, the high priest, for he and his sons and their descendants would have the solemn responsibility of caring for the lampstand, trimming the wicks, adding the sacred oil, and making sure the light was shining. (See Ex. 25:31-40; 27:20-21; 37:17-24; Lev. 24:1-3.)

Since there were no windows in the holy place, the only source of light was the golden lampstand that stood to the left of the incense altar before the veil. We aren't given the dimensions of the lampstand, but we are given a description. It was hammered out of one piece of pure gold, weighing about seventy-five pounds, with six branches and a central shaft. The branches were decorated with beautiful "buds and blossoms" (Ex. 25:33, NIV). At the end of each of the branches and the central shaft was a lamp that burned olive oil provided by the people of Israel (27:20-21).[3]

Aaron no doubt took the fire from the altar when he lit the seven lamps. From then on, it was the duty of Aaron and his sons to trim the wicks and replenish the oil each morning and evening when they offered the incense on the altar (30:7-8).

Without this light, the priests couldn't see to minister in the holy place. The instructions here added one new feature: Aaron was to turn the lamps "forward on the lampstand" (Num. 8:3, NIV) so that the light would shine on the table of showbread and be diffused throughout the holy place.

What did this lampstand signify? Since the tabernacle, its furnishings, and its service speak of the person and work of Jesus Christ (Heb. 9), the lampstand is certainly a symbol of Jesus Christ the Light of the world (John 8:12). "God is light" (1 John 1:5), and it's only through His revelation that we can see and understand spiritual truth.

The lampstand was a reminder to the priests that Israel was called to be a light to the Gentile world (Isa. 42:6; 49:6). Unless the people obeyed God and worshiped Him as He commanded, Israel's light of witness would become dim and eventually go out. That's just what happened, and part of the blame lay with the priests (Lam. 4:13). Only God could see the priests as they ministered in the holy place, but that should have been enough to motivate them to be obedient and reverent.

But before we pass judgment on Israel, how bright and far-reaching is the witness light of the churches? "Do everything without complaining or arguing, so that you may become blameless and pure, children of God without fault in a crooked and depraved generation, in which you shine like stars in the universe, as you hold out the word of life" (Phil. 2:14-16, NKJV; see Matt. 5:14-16). Israel was represented by one lampstand, but local churches are pictured as individual lampstands, with Jesus in their midst, examining them and giving His people warning and counsel (Rev. 1:12-20). If a church's light isn't shining as it should, the Lord could remove the lampstand (2:5). He would rather that there be no church in a city than that the church not love Him and therefore give false witness.

The oil for the lamps is a symbol of the Holy Spirit of God who alone can empower us to witness effectively for Christ (Zech. 4:1-4; Acts 1:8). A church that is filled with the Spirit can face opposition and continue to bear witness courageously to Jesus

Christ (Acts 4:23-33).

2. Dedicating the Levites (Num. 8:5-16)

If Aaron and his sons were the "official clergy" in the camp, serving at the altar and in the tabernacle, then the Levites were the "dedicated laity" who assisted the priests in their ministry. They were taken "from among the children of Israel" (vv. 6, 14, 16, 19) as substitutes for the firstborn males who belonged to the Lord (vv. 16-18; see 3:40-51 and Ex. 13). The Levites belonged to the Lord (Num. 8:14) and He gave them to the priests as His special gift (v. 19). The Levites cared for the tabernacle, took the structure down for each march, carried it during the march, and then erected it again in the new location.

Since they were serving God at the tabernacle, the Levites had to be set apart for the Lord. First, they were cleansed by water (vv. 5-7), but unlike the priests, were merely sprinkled and not washed all over (Ex. 29:4). It is likely that Moses and Aaron sprinkled the 22,000 Levites (Num. 3:39) collectively and not as a group. For further cleansing, the Levites were required to shave their bodies (see Lev. 14:8-9) and wash their clothes. (When consecrated to God, the priests were given special clothes to wear and weren't required to shave. See Ex. 25:5-9.)[4]

The Levites were presented to God as "living sacrifices" (Num. 8:8-14; see Rom. 12:1). The leaders of the tribes, representing the whole nation, put their hands on the Levites as an act of dedication, as though saying, "You are our substitutes, serving God on our behalf." In turn, the Levites put their hands on the two young bulls, one as a sin offering and the other as a burnt offering. It wasn't enough to purified by washing; it was also necessary that there be cleansing by blood. The burnt offering spoke of their total dedication to the Lord.

Once these prescribed acts had been completed, the Levites were permitted to begin serving the Lord and assisting the priests in their various ministries at the tabernacle (Num. 8:15-26). Numbers 4:3 states that their work began when they were thirty years old, but 8:24 gives twenty-five as the age. It's probable that the Levites had a five-year apprenticeship before entering into the full ministry at the tabernacle, because there was certainly a great deal to learn. When Levites turned fifty, they were released from the more strenuous duties but were still permitted to assist the priests as needed.[5]

Some practical principles relating to Christian service emerge from the consecration of the Levites. First of all, it is God who chooses, equips, and consecrates His people for spiritual service, and we must accept His will. The priests were in charge of the tabernacle ministry and the Levites assisted them. Every priest had to come from Aaron's family, and no Levite was allowed to take the place of a priest. Levites were not permitted to serve at the altar, wear the priestly garments, or enter the sanctuary (3:10, 38; 4:15-20; 18:1-7; Ex. 28:1; 29:9).

These distinctions in no way disparaged the Levites or minimized the importance of their work. Later, when some of the Levites tried to invade the priesthood, God judged them severely (Num. 16–17). It was no cause for pride to be a priest and no reason for shame to be a Levite, for all that we have comes from the gracious heart of God (John 3:27; 1 Cor. 4:7). There is no competition in God's service, for "each one will receive his own reward according to his own labor" (3:5-8).

A second principle is that those who serve must first of all serve the Lord and then serve His people. God's servants must be living sacrifices, "an offering unto the Lord" (Num. 8:13; Rom. 12:1). We serve the Lord by serving His people, but our orders must come from God. "Ourselves your servants for Jesus' sake" (2 Cor. 4:5). No matter what task the Lord assigns to us, it is important to His work, and we must do it cheerfully and carefully.

Finally, both the Levites and the priests were obligated to protect the sanctuary of God from intruders (Num. 8:19, and see 1:53). The priests and Levites camped immediately around the tabernacle precincts and served as a protective wall against those who wanted to invade the holy area and thus invite the judgment of God. So today, leaders in local churches must be diligent to protect the flock from those who would destroy it. "Therefore take heed to yourselves and to all the flock," was Paul's admonition to the leaders of the Ephesian church (Acts 20:28, NKJV), and he warned them that dangerous enemies would arise from both outside the church and within the congregation (vv. 29-31). God's servants must ever be on the alert and courageous to confront the enemies of God's truth.

3. Following God's guidance (Num. 9:15–10:10)

The Israelites were a pilgrim people, marching through the wilderness like an army, and they constantly needed the guidance of God. Their goal was the Promised Land, and the God who delivered them from Egypt promised to bring them into their inheritance if they would trust Him and obey His will.

Knowing the will of God and doing it is vitally important to a fulfilled and fruitful Christian life. Jeremiah was correct when he said, "O Lord, I know the way of man is not in himself; it is not in man who walks to direct his own steps" (Jer. 10:23). The child of God who fails to say, "If the Lord will," is destined for disappointment and failure (James 4:13-17).

To assist us today in determining and doing God's will, we have the Holy Spirit within us (Rom. 8:26-27; Acts 16:6-7), the Word of God before us (Ps. 119:105), and the interceding Savior above us who providentially works on our behalf (Rom. 8:28-34). To guide Israel in their journey, God gave them the pillar of cloud by day and the pillar of fire by night (Num. 9:15-23); and to announce the will of God to the people, He ordered the priests to blow two silver trumpets (10:1-10).

The pillar of cloud and fire (Num. 9:15-23). This miraculous pillar first appeared at the Exodus (Ex. 13:21-22) and it remained with Israel throughout their journey (Neh. 9:19).[6] When the Israelites set up camp, the pillar hovered over the tabernacle at the center of the camp, reminding the people day and night that their God abode with them (Num. 9:17; this is the Hebrew word *shekinah*) and would guide them a day at a time, a step at a time. It must have been an awesome sight!

Seven times in this paragraph you find the phrase "the commandment of the Lord" (vv. 18, 20, 23). The movements of the pillar were ordered by the Lord; He didn't ask for the counsel of the leaders or the people (Isa. 40:13-14). Nor were the people of God able to predict what God would do next. The pillar might linger overnight and then move in the morning, or it might stay two days, a month, or even a year. But no matter when the pillar moved, by day or by night, the Jews had to be ready to pack up and follow.

It's interesting to note that this miraculous pillar brought light to the people of Israel but darkness to their enemies (Ex. 14:19-20). In this respect, it symbolizes the Word of God, because those who don't know Christ by faith simply can't understand what the Word is saying (1 Cor. 3:12-16). In order to know the mind of God, we must submit to the will of God, and the first step is to put saving faith in Jesus Christ (Eph. 2:8-9). Then you move out of darkness and into God's wonderful light (John 3:18-21; 1 Peter 2:9; 2 Cor. 4:6; Col. 1:13).

The priests and Levites, who lived near the tabernacle, probably assigned people to keep watch day and night so they would know when the pillar was moving. If we sincerely want to do the will of God, we must keep our eyes open and be alert at all times. The New Testament word for this attitude of alertness and expectancy is "watch" (Matt. 24:42; 25:13; 1 Cor. 16:13; 1 Thes. 5:6; 1 Peter 4:7).

Jesus called Himself "the Light of the world" (John 8:12), and He promised those who followed (trusted) Him that they would never walk in darkness. It's a great privilege to "walk in the light" and enjoy fellowship with God and God's people (1 John 1:4-10). To walk in darkness means to be out of the will of God, apart from the blessing of God, and in danger of the discipline of God. Why live in the shadows or in the darkness when you can have God's smiling face shining on you? (Num. 6:24-26)

The silver trumpets (10:1-10).[7] These two instruments were blown by the priests, not the Levites, although the Levites became the official musicians for the nation (1 Chron. 23:30;

25:1-3). These two trumpets were used, not to accompany worship, but to communicate orders quickly to the camp of Israel.[8] Not only did the leaders and people have to keep their eyes open and pay attention to the pillar over the tabernacle, but they also had to keep their ears open for the sound of the trumpets.

If Moses wanted to call an assembly of the people or the leaders, the trumpet blast would give the proper signal. Two trumpets would call the people, one trumpet would call the leaders. When it was time for the camp to move, the trumpets would give the signal for each set of three tribes to march, beginning with Judah, Issachar, and Zebulun at the east end of the tabernacle. The trumpets would also sound an alarm that commanded the soldiers to prepare for battle (Num. 31:1-6; 2 Chron. 13:13-15). Numbers 10:9 describes this trumpet blast as a prayer before God that He would give His people success in battle.

But even after the nation settled in the Promised Land, the blowing of the trumpets was important to remind them of the special festivals that were a part of their religious calendar (v. 10). The Feast of Trumpets ushered in the special religious events of the seventh month: the Day of Atonement and the Feast of Tabernacles (29:1ff; Lev. 23:23-43; Ps. 81:3). The blowing of trumpets announced the special celebrations of the Jewish people, including the beginning of the Year of Jubilee (Lev. 25:8-12).

Like the Old Testament people of God, the children of God today are awaiting "the sound of the trumpet" that signals our gathering together to Jesus as well as God's declaration of war against a wicked world ready for judgment (1 Thes. 4:13-18; 1 Cor. 15:51-57). Until that hour, we remain a pilgrim people in this wilderness world, following His directions and serving Him faithfully.

FOUR

Marching to Moab

The people of Israel camped at Mount Sinai about eleven months. They arrived there in the third month after their deliverance from Egypt (Ex. 19:1), and it was now the second month of the second year. During that time, God's Law had been announced and the tabernacle had been constructed and dedicated. Moses had consecrated the priests and Levites, counted the soldiers, and organized the tribes. Israel was now a nation ready for action.

However, Israel's history for the next thirty-eight years (Num. 10:11–22:1) is for the most part a record of unbelief and failure. They were years during which the people opposed Moses and rebelled against God's will. Because of their disobedience at Kadesh-Barnea, Israel wandered in the wilderness for thirty-eight years, leaving behind a trail of graves as the older generation died off. Of that generation, only Joshua and Caleb survived to enter Canaan.

In contrast, the first ten chapters of Numbers have recorded the activities of a nation obeying the Lord. "And the children of Israel did according to all that the Lord commanded Moses, so did they" (1:54) is a theme often repeated in these chapters

(2:34; 3:16, 51; 4:49; 5:4; 8:3, 20, 22; 9:5, 23). In obeying God, Israel had everything to gain and nothing to lose; yet they refused to trust Him and follow His commandments. It's not until Numbers 26 that the picture changes, when Moses takes a census of the new generation and prepares them to enter the land, conquer the enemy, and claim their inheritance.

Let's consider three scenes in the life of Israel as the nation began its journey, and let's learn what it means to know God's will and do it.

1. Marching at God's command (Num. 10:11-36)

The cloud over the tabernacle moved, the priests blew the trumpets, the priests and Levites dismantled the tabernacle, and the people prepared to march. They had been comfortable while at Sinai, living in the same place for nearly a year and not having to face the rigors of a daily march. God's great victory over Egypt was fresh in their minds, and each morning when they gathered the manna, they were reminded of God's gracious provision for their every need.

But their inheritance wasn't Mount Sinai; it was the Promised Land, "the land of milk and honey" that God had promised His people. It was time for them to move. The more comfortable we become, the less we welcome change; and yet there's no growth without challenge and there's no challenge without change. Comfort usually leads to complacency, and complacency is the enemy of character and spiritual growth. In each new experience of life, one of two things happens: either we trust God and He brings out the best in us, or we disobey God and Satan brings out the worst in us.

Marching in order (Num. 10:11-28). The tribes already had their leaders (Num. 1) and knew the marching order (Num. 2), so all that the priests had to do was sound the trumpets and signal when each tribe should move out and join the procession. The ark of the covenant led the way, carried by the Levites and following the pillar of cloud (10:33-36; Neh. 9:12; Ps. 78:14). The ark was the throne of God (80:1; 99:1, NIV), and the Lord was sovereign over His people. He led the way. "You led Your people like a flock by the hand of Moses and Aaron" (77:20, NKJV).

Judah, Issachar, and Zebulun were at the head of the march, followed by the Gershonites and Merarites carrying the tabernacle proper. Next were Reuben, Simeon, and Gad, followed by the Kohathites bearing the tabernacle furniture at the heart of the procession. It was the safest place for those valuable furnishings. The tribes of Ephraim, Manasseh, and Benjamin came next, and then Dan, Asher, and Naphtali. The "mixed multitude" that did not belong to any tribe brought up the rear (Num. 11:4; Ex. 12:38).

Where each tribe marched in the procession wasn't an option; it was an obligation, an order from Almighty God. If the tribe of Dan or Asher grew tired of being at the end of the march and asked to take the lead, Moses would have refused their request, for the will of God in this matter wasn't negotiable. The people of Israel weren't on a pleasure trip, looking at the scenery. They were an army invading enemy territory and commanded by the Lord of Hosts. Each tribe was a division in the Lord's army (Num. 28; "divisions," NIV), and each division had to be in its proper place.

Inviting others to come (Num. 10:29-32). Hobab was Moses' brother-in-law, the son of Raguel, who was also know as Reuel and Jethro (Ex. 2:15-3:1).[1] It's likely that Jethro was now dead and Hobab was head of the family. Moses wanted his in-laws to travel with Israel and enjoy the blessings God had promised His people, but Hobab declined the offer. He preferred to stay in his own land with his own people. Why should he sacrifice comfort and security for an unknown future?

But Moses knew that Jehovah was with Israel and that the future lay with those who trusted Him and obeyed His laws. Perhaps that's why Moses added a special challenge to his invitation: because of Hobab's knowledge of the terrain, he could assist Israel in its wilderness journey. Hobab must have agreed to the proposal, because years later we find his descendants living with the

Israelites (Jud. 1:16; 4:11). Certainly they were better off being a part of the people of God.

Bible students disagree over whether Moses was right or wrong when he asked Hobab to be Israel's "eyes" as they traveled in the wilderness. After all, wasn't the nation being led by the pillar of cloud and the ark of the Lord? And didn't God speak to Moses personally and reveal His will to him? Then why draft a human guide when they had so much help from heaven?

But divine providence doesn't minimize or destroy human ability or responsibility. Israel didn't need Hobab to tell them where to march or where to camp; God would do that. But Hobab's knowledge of the land would assist them in making other decisions as they moved from place to place. Charles Spurgeon said: "We ought to learn from this, I think, that while we ever seek the guidance of God in providence, yet we may frequently find direction and guidance in the use of our own common sense, our own discretion with which the Lord has endowed us."[2] We don't "lean on" our own understanding (Prov. 3:5-6), but neither do we ignore it. God wants us to act intelligently as well as believingly, and the spiritually minded Christian knows how to use both heart and mind in discerning God's will (Rom. 12:2).

But let's not miss the main thrust of what Moses did: He invited others to come with Israel to enjoy the blessings God had prepared for them. The church today is a pilgrim people in this world (1 Peter 1:1; 2:11), traveling toward heaven, and it's our privilege to invite others to come along with us. The journey isn't easy, but God is blessing His people now and will bless them forever. How many have we invited lately?

Glorifying the Lord (Num. 10:33-36). The suggestion here is that Moses and Aaron marched ahead of the tribes, just behind the ark. Each time the pillar of cloud signaled a move and the tribes were assembled, Moses prayed to God for guidance and victory; and when the nation stopped to camp, he prayed that God's presence would again rest with His people at the tabernacle. The ark would be put into the holy of holies and the pillar of fire would rest over the tent.[3]

No matter how many times the Israelites started and stopped in their journey, Moses repeated these prayers.[4] He wanted the people to know that God, not Moses, was in charge of the nation, and that Israel was an army that depended on the Lord for victory. Like the invocation and benediction at a church worship service, these prayers became familiar to the Jews, *but these brief prayers were essential to Israel's well-being as a nation.* Moses put God first in the life of the people; and had the Jews paid attention to this, they would have avoided the sins that later brought them so much sorrow.

2. Complaining to God's servant (Num. 11:1-35)

So sinful is the human heart that it's prone to forget God's blessings, ignore God's promises, and find fault with God's providence. "Oh that men would praise the Lord for His goodness, and for His wonderful works to the children of men!" (Ps. 107:8, 15, 21, 31)

The Jews complain (Num. 11:1-3). History repeats itself. Three days after the great praise service by the Red Sea, the Jews complained against Moses and God because they didn't have water to drink (Ex. 15:22-27). Now, three days after leaving Sinai (Num. 10:33), the Jews complain again. It takes faith to be able to accept God's providential leading (Rom. 8:28), and Israel's faith wasn't very strong.

Since the people had been camped in one location for nearly a year, perhaps the demands of the journey discouraged them, along with the monotony of the terrain. The NIV translates Numbers 11:1, "Now the people complained about their hardships." Whatever the cause, God heard their sinful words, became angry, and killed the ungrateful people.[5] "The fire of the Lord" could describe lightning (Ex. 9:23-24), and the fact that the judgment fell on people dwelling in the outskirts of the camp indicates that perhaps the "mixed multitude" was the cause of the complaining (Num. 11:4).

How often in my own pastoral ministry I've seen verse 2

demonstrated: The people who complain the most about God and their spiritual leaders end up coming to those leaders for help! How gracious Moses was to intercede on their behalf, and how like our Lord Jesus Christ! "Father, forgive them; for they know not what they do" (Luke 23:34). More than once when Israel sinned, it was the intercession of Moses that stayed God's hand of judgment. On one occasion, Moses even offered to die so that Israel might be spared (Ex. 32:30-35).

The mixed multitude complains (Num. 11:4-9). This is the only place in the Old Testament where the Hebrew word *'asapsup* is used, and it describes a "rabble," the "riffraff" that accompanied the Jews when they left Egypt (Ex. 12:38).[6] Why they left Egypt isn't explained. Some of them may have been afraid that more judgments were coming and the safest course was to go with the Jews (9:20). Some servants and slaves may have seen in Israel's departure an opportunity to get out of Egypt while people were busy burying their dead. Others may have had good intentions, but because they had no faith in the Lord, their hearts were never changed (Heb. 4:1-2).

Whatever their origin, the "mixed multitude" caused Moses and the people of Israel a great deal of trouble, and a similar group is creating problems for God's servants and people today. In the Parable of the Tares (Matt. 13:24-30, 36-43), Jesus taught that wherever the Lord "plants" His true children, the devil comes along and plants counterfeits. Satan is an imitator and an infiltrator (Jude 4; 2 Peter 2:1-2), which explains why Paul warned the church about "false brethren" (Gal. 2:4; 2 Cor. 11:26), false ministers (v. 13ff), and a false gospel (Gal. 1:6-9).

Over these many years of ministry, I've learned that it isn't enemies *outside* the local church who do the damage but counterfeiters who get *inside* the church fellowship (Acts 20:28-30; 3 John 9-11). These intruders might march with the church crowd and act like they are God's people, but they don't have an appetite for spiritual things; and eventually their true allegiance is revealed (1 John 2:18-19).

The Jews experienced a miracle six mornings a week when the

"bread of heaven" (Pss. 78:24; 105:40) fell in the camp and provided all the nourishment they needed for the day. Perhaps influenced by the mixed multitude, many of the Jews got tired of their diet and tried to improve on God's recipe (Num. 11:8). They wanted instead the food they had enjoyed in Egypt. They forgot the bondage of Egypt and remembered only the things that pleased the flesh!

How tragic it is when professed believers in churches crave substitutes from the world instead of desiring the heavenly manna of the Word of God (John 6:66-69; Matt. 4:4). In trying to attract and please the "mixed multitude," churches have turned their sanctuaries into theaters and their ministries into performances, and worship has become entertainment. Paul had to deal with this crowd in his day (Phil. 3:17-21), so it's nothing new.

However, it's a serious thing to complain against the Lord, attack His servants, and ask for "religious substitutes" that satisfy our fleshly desires. These murmurers in Israel were eventually judged by God and used by Paul as a warning to the churches today (1 Cor. 10:10). "Do all things without murmurings and disputings" (Phil. 2:14). An unthankful heart makes it easier for people to commit all kinds of sins (Rom. 1:21ff).

Moses laments his calling (Num. 11:10-15). Moses had been singing triumphantly about the Lord (10:35-36), but now he is lamenting bitterly the work God called him to do. Few things discourage God's servants more than people criticizing them unjustly and complaining about the blessings the Lord has given.[7] This is the first of two occasions when the attitude of the people caused Moses to sin (see 20:1-13). Knowing as we do how ungrateful and hardhearted the people of Israel were, we wonder that Moses wasn't discouraged more often!

It's sad to see a great man of God ask God to take his life because he feels that his divine calling is a heavy burden by which God has afflicted him and made him wretched. Moses lost his perspective and got his eyes off the Lord and on himself, something that's easy to do in the difficult experiences of life. His "I am not able" (11:14) reminds us of when God called Moses and assured him of His help (Ex. 3:11-12). But at least Moses took his burden to the Lord and accepted God's counsel (1 Peter 5:7).

Moses receives God's help (Num. 11:16-35). The Lord helped Moses solve two difficult problems: how to pastor so many people and how to provide meat for all the people. Both problems stemmed from Israel's sojourn in Egypt where they developed appetites for the diet of their masters. The Jews forgot the slavery and remembered only the "free" food.

As for the first problem (vv. 16-17, 24-30), God commanded Moses to select seventy godly elders to assist him in the spiritual oversight of the camp. Moses already had leaders to help the people settle their personal disputes (Ex. 18), but these new leaders would have more of a spiritual ministry to the people. After all, the heart of every problem is the problem in the heart, and unless people's hearts are changed by the Lord, their character and conduct will never change.

Sixty-eight of the seventy men gathered at the tabernacle, and God gave them the power of the Spirit so they could assist Moses in his work.[8] Their worship of God was evidence that they truly had received the Spirit (see Acts 2:11; 10:44-46; 19:1-7; Eph. 5:18-20). Why Eldad and Medad were not in the meeting isn't explained, but since they weren't disciplined by God, we assume their absence wasn't a serious matter. At least they didn't miss out on any of the blessing. Joshua was upset about their receiving the Spirit but Moses was grateful. He seems to have regained his usual composure and attitude of generosity when he said, "Would God that all the Lord's people were prophets, and that the Lord would put His Spirit upon them!"

Moses wasn't the only servant of God to face this problem of "spiritual exclusiveness." John the Baptist faced it (John 3:26-30), and so did Jesus (Luke 9:46-50) and Paul (Phil. 1:15-18). However, Joshua felt that Moses and God were losing something by allowing these two men to receive the Spirit. The first time we meet Joshua in Scripture, he is leading the army of Israel in victory over the Amalekites (Ex. 17:8-16). Then we see

48

him on Mount Sinai with Moses (24:13; 32:17), and now we learn that he is Moses' servant (Num. 11:28). Later, he will become Moses' successor.

The second problem had to do with finding enough meat to feed the nation (vv. 18-23, 31-35; see Ex. 16:1-13). The Jews certainly weren't going to slaughter their flocks and herds because that would have left them destitute. By sending a wind, God brought quail right to the camp, three feet above the ground; and the Jews spent two days and a night capturing and killing the birds.[9] Ten homers (Num. 11:32) would be about sixty bushels of meat! But God told them they would have enough meat to eat for a month (vv. 19-20).

When God really wants to judge people, He lets them have their own way (Rom. 1:24, 26, 28). "So He gave them what they asked for, but He sent a plague along with it" (Ps. 106:15, NLT). The Jews began to devour the meat, happy that their craving was being satisfied; but then God's judgment struck and many of them died (Num. 11:33; Ps. 78:23-31; 1 Cor. 10:10). Moses called the place "the graves of lust," and those graves were a monument to the danger of praying, "Not Thy will but my will be done."

The Lord had warned Israel that the way they treated the daily manna would be a test of their obedience to His Word (Ex. 16:4; Deut. 8:3). In rejecting the manna, Israel really rejected the Lord (Num. 11:20, NIV), and it was this rebellious attitude that invited the judgment of God. This reminds us that the way we treat God's Word is the way we treat the Lord Himself. To ignore the Word, treat it carelessly, or willfully disobey it is to ask for the discipline of God (Heb. 12:5-11). Instead of feeding on the things of the world that bring death, let's cultivate an appetite for the holy Word of God (Job 23:12; Ps. 1:1; Jer. 15:16; Matt. 4:4; Luke 10:38-42; 1 Peter 2:1-3).

3. Delaying because of God's discipline (Num. 12:1-16)
People in places of spiritual leadership know that problems usually come in clusters of twos or threes. Why? Because Satan is

alive and busy (1 Peter 5:8-9) and sinful human nature fights the holy will of God (Gal. 5:16-17). Just about the time the Lord helps you settle one crisis, another one appears.

The false accusation (Num. 12:1-3). Moses, Aaron, and Miriam were a team sent by God to help lead the nation of Israel (Micah 6:4). God had used Miriam to save her younger brother's life (Ex. 2:1-10), and she was also a prophetess who led the Jewish women in praising God (15:20-21).[10] Aaron was the elder brother in the family (Ex. 7:7), appointed by God not only to assist Moses in confronting Pharaoh (4:10-17) but also to serve as the first high priest. Everybody in Israel knew that Moses, Aaron, and Miriam were God's chosen servants, but that Moses was the leader.

Three pieces of evidence lead to the conclusion that Miriam was the leader in this family rebellion: she is mentioned first in Numbers 12:1; the verb "spoke" is feminine in form, and Miriam alone was disciplined by the Lord. She didn't begin her assault by accusing Moses of usurping authority but by differing with him over his wife. (Most people who accuse God's servants rarely give the real reasons for their disagreements.) It's likely that Zipporah had died and Moses had taken a new wife, and perhaps Miriam felt threatened by her. Also, when the Lord sent the Spirit upon the seventy elders, Miriam may have felt an erosion of her own authority.

As long as Moses didn't marry a woman from one of the Canaanite nations, his marriage was acceptable to the Lord (Ex. 34:12-16). In Scripture, "Cush" usually refers to a people who lived near Egypt, but the KJV wrongly translates the Hebrew word "Ethiopia." For that reason, some have taught that the new wife belonged to a different race and therefore was unacceptable. According to William S. LaSor, "There is no evidence, either in the Bible or in extrabiblical material, to support the view that Ham or any of his descendants was negroid."[11]

Miriam finally got around to her real complaint: Was Moses the only spokesperson for God? Didn't Miriam and Aaron also have the right to declare God's Word? In questioning Moses' authority and God's will, Miriam and Aaron were acting just like the people of Israel! However, Moses didn't answer them or try to vindicate himself; he left his defense to the Lord. This was one evidence of his meekness; meekness is not weakness: it's power under control.[12]

The swift judgment (Num. 12:4-10). God heard their words, saw the evil motives in their hearts, and acted swiftly lest their sin spread among the people, because when leaders sin, the consequences can be disastrous. Note that in verse 4 the three names are reversed from the order in verse 1. God put Moses first! He called all three to the tabernacle, spoke to the two (Miriam and Aaron), and pronounced judgment on the one—Miriam.

God made it clear that Moses was more than a prophet, because God communicated with him personally and even revealed His glory to him (Ex. 19:16-19; 24:17-18; 34:5-11). Miriam and Aaron each had their assigned ministries, but Moses was God's chosen leader for Israel and nobody could take his place. It was God who gave Moses his position and authority, and it was wicked for Miriam to challenge her brother. In judgment, God afflicted Miriam with leprosy.

The impassioned plea (Num. 12:11-13). Aaron knew the significance of the leprosy and he begged Moses to intercede for Miriam and himself, for the pronouns are plural: "We have sinned." Aaron was the interceding high priest for Israel and yet he needed an intercessor! As further evidence of his meekness, Moses prayed for his sister; and the Lord did remove the affliction.

The embarrassing delay (Num. 12:14-16). Though Miriam was healed, she had to remain outside the camp for seven days (see Lev. 13:1-6; 14:1-8; 15:8) because she had been defiled. This meant shame for Miriam, for the whole camp knew what had happened. But it also meant delay for the people, for the camp had to wait for her restoration before it could move. The rebellious sinner is always a cause of holding back the progress of God's people.

It's a serious thing to be a spiritual leader, for the greater the honor, the greater the responsibility. It's also a serious thing to try to usurp the authority God has given to others. "Those [elders] who are sinning rebuke in the presence of all, that the rest also may fear" (1 Tim. 5:20, NKJV). Jesus warned that our enemies might be those from our own household (Matt. 10:34-36; Micah 7:6).

"Obey them that have the rule over you, and submit yourselves; for they watch for your souls, as they that must give account, that they may do it with joy, and not with grief; for that is unprofitable for you" (Heb. 13:17).

"Remember what the Lord your God did to Miriam on the way when you came out of Egypt" (Deut. 24:9, NKJV).

FIVE

Crisis at Kadesh

At Kadesh-Barnea, on the border of Canaan, the people of Israel foolishly forfeited their opportunity to enter the Promised Land and claim their inheritance. This tragic failure has made the name "Kadesh" a synonym for defeat and lost opportunity. Israel's downfall at Kadesh is a reminder to us today that it's a dangerous thing to trifle with the will of God. You may end up spending the rest of your life wandering around, just waiting to die.

In spite of what some of our hymns declare, Canaan is not a picture of heaven. Certainly there won't be any battles in heaven! Rather, Canaan is a picture of the inheritance God has planned for each of His children today, the work He wants us to do, and the places He wants us to occupy. Paul called it "good works, which God prepared beforehand that we should walk in them" (Eph. 2:10, NKJV). The Lord has a perfect plan for each of His children, but we can claim these blessings only by faith and obedience.

Like the people of Israel centuries ago, many believers today walk by sight and not by faith, and therefore they fail to enjoy the good things God has for them. They can't say with David,

"The lines have fallen to me in pleasant places; yes, I have a good inheritance" (Ps. 16:6, NKJV). What did Israel do at Kadesh that brought about their shameful defeat? They committed at least five blatant sins, and God's children today can commit those same sins and suffer the same kind of shameful defeat.

1. Doubting God's Word (Num. 13:1-25)

God delivered His people from Egypt that they might enter the Promised Land and enjoy the blessings prepared for them. Forty years later, Moses reminded the new generation, "And He brought us out from there [Egypt], that He might bring us in, to give us the land which He swore to give unto our fathers" (Deut. 6:23; see Ezek. 20:6). The Lord had promised the land to the descendants of Abraham, Isaac, and Jacob (Gen. 12:7; 13:15; 17:8; 28:13; 35:12) and had reaffirmed that promise through Moses (Ex. 3:8, 17; 6:4, 8; 13:5; 33:3).

But even more, the Lord had reminded the people of His promise when they broke camp at Sinai (Deut. 1:6-8) and when they arrived at Kadesh (vv. 20-21). God's promise was Israel's title deed to the land as well as His guarantee that they would defeat their enemies. God's promise was all Israel needed, but the nation doubted God's Word and began to walk by sight instead of by faith.

They took their first wavering step of doubt when they asked Moses to let them search out the land before the entire nation went in to engage the enemy in battle (Deut. 1:22; James 1:5-8). Moses endorsed their request (Deut. 1:23) and got permission from the Lord to carry out the plan (Num. 13:1-3). However, it appears that God was letting the Jews have their own way, not because their way was the right way, but because He wanted to teach them a lesson. They needed to learn to trust the Word of God and do the will of God His way and not their own way (Prov. 3:5-6).

The twelve spies chosen were different men from the leaders named in Numbers 1–2; 7; and 10. These spies had to be younger men who could endure the rigors and dangers involved in reconnoitering the land. We meet Caleb for the first time in 13:6, but he'll be mentioned thirty-one more times in the Old Testament. He and Joshua were the only members of the older generation to enter the Promised Land. The rest of them died in the wilderness.

We first meet Joshua in Scripture as Israel's general (Ex. 17:8-16), defeating the Amalekites, and then as the servant of Moses (24:13; Num. 11:28). He eventually became Moses' successor (27:15-20) and led Israel in their conquest of the Promised Land. His original name was Hoshea, which means "salvation," but Moses changed it to "Joshua" which means "Jehovah is salvation." It was the kind of name that would encourage the faith of a soldier and remind him that the Lord was fighting for him.

The twelve spies traveled about 500 miles during the forty days of their survey of Canaan, but they discovered nothing that God hadn't already told them! They already knew the names of the pagan nations that lived in the land (Gen. 15:18-21), that it was a good land (Ex. 3:8) and a rich land flowing with milk and honey (vv. 8, 17). They saw the incredible fruit of the land and brought back a huge bunch of grapes for the people to see. They even visited Hebron, where the patriarchs of Israel were buried with their wives (Num. 13:22; Gen. 23:2, 19; 49:29-31; 50:13). Did the reminder of the faith of Abraham, Isaac, Jacob, and Joseph encourage their own trust in God? For ten of the spies, the answer is no.

The survey of the land may have been a good idea from a conventional military point of view, but not from a spiritual point of view. God had already given them the land and had commanded them to go in and take it. He had promised them victory, so all they had to do was "trust and obey." The Lord would go before them and scatter His enemies (Num. 10:33-36), but His people had to follow by faith. That was where they failed. They doubted that God was able to keep His promises and give them the land.

2. Discouraging God's people (Num. 13:26-33; Deut. 1:26-28)

Someone has defined a committee as "a group of people who

individually can do nothing and collectively decide nothing can be done." Because they lacked faith, all the spies except Caleb and Joshua were discouraged at the prospect of entering the land and fighting the enemy, and their discouragement quickly spread throughout the camp. Doubt had turned into unbelief, and unbelief is rebellion against God (Num. 14:9; Heb. 3:16-19).

It's interesting how the ten spies identified Canaan as "the land to which you sent us" (Num. 13:27) and "the land through which we have gone" (v. 32), but not as "the land the Lord our God is giving us." Because these ten men were walking by sight, they didn't really believe God's promises. They looked at the people of the land and saw giants; they looked at the Canaanite cities and saw high walls and locked gates; and they looked at themselves and saw grasshoppers. If only they had looked by faith to God, they would have seen the One who was able to conquer every enemy and who sees the nations of the world as grasshoppers (Isa. 40:22). "We are not able" is the cry of unbelief (Num. 13:31), but, "Our God is able" is the affirmation of faith (Dan. 3:17; see Phil. 4:13).

What John Gardner said about the political arena can be applied to the spiritual arena and the Christian's walk of faith: "We are continually faced with a series of great opportunities brilliantly disguised as insoluble problems." A faith that can't be tested can't be trusted, and God tests our faith to help us make sure it's genuine (1 Peter 1:1-9) and to help make it grow. "Faith comes first to the hearing ear," said A.W. Tozer, "not to the cogitating mind." "So then faith comes by hearing, and hearing by the word of God" (Rom. 10:17, NKJV).

To the unbelieving world, it's unreasonable for anybody to trust a God they've never seen or heard, but we have all the evidence we need to convince us that God is dependable and has the power to accomplish what He says He will do. What He promises, He is able to perform (Rom. 4:21). Israel had seen what the Lord did to the Egyptians and the Amalekites (Ex. 17:8-16), and they had every assurance that He would never fail His people.

Unbelief is serious because it challenges the character of God and rebels against the will of God. "But without faith it is impossible to please [God]" (Heb. 11:6). "For whatever is not of faith is sin" (Rom. 14:23). Moses reminded the people of what God had already done for them (Deut. 1:29-33), but they wouldn't stop complaining. They were sure that the best thing to do was return to Egypt and go back into bondage.

3. Defying God's will (Num. 14:1-10)

In the camp of Israel, unbelief and discouragement spread rapidly from heart to heart, and before long "all the congregation lifted up their voice, and cried; and the people wept that night" (v. 1, and note vv. 2 and 10). The next day, the whole congregation criticized Moses and Aaron and lamented the fact that the nation hadn't perished in Egypt or in the wilderness. When your eyes are on yourself and your circumstances, you lose your perspective and say and do ridiculous things.

However, the Jews had a long record of complaining against the Lord and their leaders, and being judged for it. Their murmuring began on the night of the Exodus when they were sure Pharaoh's army was going to kill them (Ex. 14:10-14). As Israel entered the wilderness of Shur, they complained because they didn't have water to drink (15:22-27), and then they murmured because they missed the delicious meals that were provided in Egypt (Ex. 16). "Would that we had died in the land of Egypt!" was their favorite lament. At Rephidim, the people were ready to stone Moses because they had no water (17:1-7), and at Taberah some of the people complained and were killed by fire (Num. 11:1-3). Shortly after that, the mixed multitude incited the Jews to ask for meat to eat, and Moses became so discouraged he wanted to die (vv. 4ff).

In most churches, there are two or three chronic complainers who plague the spiritual leaders and sometime must be disciplined; but here was an entire nation weeping over a plight that they had caused by their own unbelief! They didn't admit their own failings; instead, they blamed God and decided to choose a new leader and return to Egypt (14:3-4). This was rebellion against the will of God.

When the child of God is in the will of God, there is no place for complaining, even if the circumstances are difficult. The will of God will never lead us where the grace of God can't provide for us or the power of God protect us. If our daily prayer is, "Thy will be done," and if we walk in obedience to God's will, then what is there to complain about? A complaining spirit is evidence of an ungrateful heart and an unsurrendered will. By our grumbling, we're daring to say that we know more than God does about what's best for His people! "Do everything without complaining or arguing" (Phil. 2:14, NIV; and see 1 Cor. 10:10).

There were four men of faith in the camp—Moses, Aaron, Caleb, and Joshua—and they tried to change the situation. Moses and Aaron fell on their faces and interceded with God, something they would do often in the years ahead (see Num. 16:4, 22, 45; 20:6; 22:31), but Caleb and Joshua spoke to the people and assured them that the Jewish army could easily take the land because God was with them. These two men saw the nation's sin for what it really was: rebellion against God.

The ten unbelieving spies argued that the land of Canaan would "eat up" the Jewish people (13:32), but Joshua and Caleb saw the Canaanites as "bread" for the Jewish army to "eat up" (14:9). The Jews didn't appreciate what Joshua and Caleb were saying and decided to stone them along with Moses and Aaron (v. 10). When we walk by sight and not by faith, we don't have sense enough to know who our real friends are, and we turn against those who can help us the most.

The will of God is the expression of the love of God for His people, for His plans come from His heart (Ps. 33:11). God's will isn't punishment, it's nourishment (John 4:31-34); not painful chains that shackle us (Ps. 2:3), but loving cords that tie us to God's heart so He can lead us in the right way (Hosea 11:4). Those who rebel against God's will are denying His wisdom, questioning His love, and tempting the Lord to discipline them. Sometimes God has to put a "bit and bridle" on rebels in order to control them (Ps. 32:8-9), and that's not enjoyable.

God wants us to know His will (Acts 22:14), understand His will (Eph. 5:17), delight in His will (Ps. 40:8), and obey His will from the heart (Eph. 6:6). As we yield to the Lord, trust Him, and obey Him, we "prove by experience" what the will of God is (Rom. 12:1-2). The Spirit of God opens up the Word of God to us and helps us discern what God wants us to do. But it's important that we are willing to obey, or He won't teach us what we need to know (John 7:17). The British Anglican minister F.W. Robertson (1816–1853) was right when he said that obedience was the organ of spiritual knowledge. If we aren't willing to obey, God isn't obligated to reveal His will to us.

4. Deserving God's judgment (Num. 14:11-38)

More than once, Israel in her pride tempted God in the wilderness, and He responded with judgment (Deut. 6:16; Pss. 78:17-18, 41, 56; 95:8-11; 106). Like a stubborn child, the Jews never seemed to learn their lesson. Instead of pleasing the Lord who had done so much for them, they provoked Him to anger and dared Him to act.

Intercession (Num. 14:11-19). As he had done when Israel worshiped the golden calf (Ex. 32), Moses interceded for the people and turned away the wrath of God. For a second time, God offered to make a new nation out of Moses and completely destroy the Jewish people (Num. 14:11), but Moses refused. It's the mark of great and godly leaders that they think only of the good of their people and not their own personal gain. In fact, Moses was willing to die for the nation rather than let God destroy it (Ex. 32:32; see Rom. 9:1-3).

Moses reasoned with God and argued first of all that His glory would be tarnished if Israel were destroyed. The nations had heard what God did in Egypt, but they would no longer fear Him if Israel were destroyed. The nations would say, "He brought Israel out of Egypt but wasn't able to bring them into the land. This means that the gods of the land of Canaan are stronger than Jehovah!" The great concern of Moses was that God be glorified before the nations.

His second argument was the covenant God had made with the patriarchs years before (Num. 14:16). The Lord had promised Abraham, Isaac, and Jacob that He would give them the land, and He could not go back on His word (Gen. 13:17; 15:7-21; 28:13; 35:12).

For his third argument, Moses pointed to the character of God and quoted what God Himself had declared to him on Mount Sinai (Num. 14:17-18; Ex. 34:6-7). Because He is a holy God, the Lord must punish sin, but because He is a gracious and merciful God, He forgives sin. How does God solve this dilemma? By giving His own Son on the cross to pay for the sins of the world. Because of the cross, God is both just and the justifier of those who trust in Christ (Rom. 3:21-31). He upholds His holy law and is true to His own character, and at the same time makes forgiveness available to sinners who repent and believe in Jesus Christ.

God in His grace and mercy forgives sin, but in His divine government He allows that sin to have its sad effects in the lives of sinners. He doesn't hold the children responsible for the sins of their parents, but children can suffer because of their parents' sins. Since many Jewish homes were comprised of three or four generations, this meant that the entire household would suffer because of the sins of the fathers.

Moses' final argument for Israel's forgiveness was the fact that the Lord had forgiven His people many times before (Num. 14:19). "He has not dealt with us according to our sins, nor punished us according to our iniquities" (Ps. 103:10, NKJV; see Ezra 9:13). The fact that God forgives us isn't an encouragement for us to go on sinning, because the Lord chastens those who rebel against Him. He forgives us so we'll fear Him (Ps. 130:4) and have no more desire to sin (John 8:10-11).

Forgiveness (Num. 14:20-22). God assured Moses that He did indeed pardon their sin (v. 20), but that He would not prevent their sin from working out its terrible destructive consequences. The rebellious Israelites weren't concerned about the glory of the

Lord, even though His glory guided them day by day and hovered over the tabernacle each night. God wanted to use Israel to magnify His glory throughout the whole earth (v. 21; Ps. 72:19; Isa. 6:3; Hab. 2:14), but they had failed miserably.

Discipline (Num. 14:23-38). God's judgment was threefold: (1) The nation would wander for thirty-eight years, thus making forty years in the wilderness, one for each day the spies had explored the land; (2) During that time, the older generation, twenty years and upward, would die and not enter the land, except for Caleb and Joshua; (3) The ten unbelieving spies died because of the evil report they delivered (vv. 36-38).

The Jews had lamented that they wanted to die in the wilderness (v. 2), and they had complained that their children would die in Canaan (v. 3); but God declared that their children would live in Canaan and the adults would die in the wilderness! Out of their own mouths, God passed judgment.[1] Be careful what you say to God when you complain, because He may take you up on it! After all, God's greatest judgment is to let people have their own way.

Moses led the world's longest funeral march, and Caleb and Joshua watched their generation die.[2] But Caleb and Joshua would be encouraged by God's promise that both of them would enter the land and enjoy their inheritance. This assurance alone would sustain them during the trying days of the nation's march, a discipline that wasn't the fault of either Caleb or Joshua. So the blessed hope of Christ's return encourages God's people today in spite of the trials we experience on our pilgrim walk.

5. Disobeying God's command (Num. 14:39-45; Deut. 1:41-46)

The day after their great failure, the Jews were supposed to start on their long march through the wilderness (Num. 14:25), but the nation refused to obey. Unbelief, a spirit of complaining, and a rebellious attitude are terrible masters that cause no end of trouble in the lives of those who cultivate them. "Pride goes before destruction, and a haughty spirit before a fall" (Prov. 16:18, NKJV).

The Israelites may have "mourned greatly" (Num. 14:39) and said, "We have sinned" (v. 40),[3] but this "mourning" was regret and not true repentance. The Jews regretted the consequences of their sins but not the sins themselves. Israel had rebelled against God and robbed Him of glory, yet they exhibited no brokenness of spirit or sorrow for sin. Unlike Moses and Aaron, they didn't fall on their faces and seek the Lord's help. Instead, they went from rebellion to presumption and tried to fight the enemy on their own.

Admitting sin isn't the same as confessing sin and turning to the Lord to seek His mercy. The Jews thought that they could make a new beginning because God had granted them forgiveness, but they were wrong. God had forgiven their sins, but He had also instituted a new plan that would delay Israel's conquest of the Promised Land for nearly forty years. An unbelieving people with an arrogant attitude could never defeat the heathen nations in Canaan. If Israel wasn't right with God, they could never claim God's help as they sought to conquer the land.[4]

Neither Moses nor the ark left the camp (see 10:33-36), the cloud didn't move from the tabernacle, and the silver trumpets didn't blow. Yet the makeshift army went out to do battle! The word translated "presumed" in 14:44 comes from a Hebrew word that means "to be lifted up," that is, "to be proud, arrogant, and swelled up with one's own importance." The soldiers' boast, "We will go up and fight," was answered by God's warning, "I will not be with you" (Deut. 1:41-42, NIV). Man's efforts without God's blessing do more harm than good, for Jesus said, "Without Me you can do nothing" (John 15:5).

The Lord's prediction came true and the Israelite army was defeated ignominiously. Not only did the Amalekites and Canaanites rout the Jewish forces as they attacked, but they chased the Jewish army over 100 miles north, as far as Hormah. It was a sad day for the descendants of Abraham, Isaac, and Jacob.

The entire experience at Kadesh-Barnea teaches us that there is no substitute for faith in God's promises and obedience to His commandments. Faith is simply obeying God in spite of how we feel, what we see, or what we think might happen. When God's people trust and obey, the Lord delights in doing wonders for them, because they glorify His name.

The agnostic American newspaper editor Henry L. Mencken defined faith as "an illogical belief in the occurrence of the impossible." Mark Twain wrote that faith was "believing what you know ain't so." Both were wrong.

Evangelist D.L. Moody said that "real true faith is man's weakness leaning on God's strength." It's taking God at His Word and proving it by obeying what He tells us to do.

That's where Israel failed.

Let's not follow their example!

SIX

A *Question of Authority*

The events described in these chapters probably occurred shortly after Israel's tragic failure at Kadesh-Barnea, and they reveal clearly that the people still hadn't learned how to trust and obey. No wonder the Lord rejected the older generation and made a new beginning with the younger generation!

God had a special word of encouragement for the younger generation: "After you enter the land I am giving you as a home" (15:1, NIV). The younger generation faced thirty-eight years of wandering, but the Lord guaranteed that they would one day enter the land and claim their inheritance. The children suffered because of the sins of their fathers and had to participate in history's longest funeral march.

The older generation of Israelites repeatedly refused to submit to the authority of God's Word as well as the authority of God's appointed leaders. Believers today commit the same sins, and the consequences are evident: divided churches, dysfunctional families, and disobedient individuals who wander from church to church but never accomplish much for the Lord. Unless we submit to God's Word and God's chosen leaders (Heb. 13:7-9, 17), we can't successfully claim our inheritance in Christ (Eph. 2:10) and accomplish what God wants us to do.

1. The authority of God's Word (Num. 15:1-41)

The Lord wanted the new generation to enter the Promised Land and enjoy it for many years, but that enjoyment depended on their obedience to His Word.[1] Moses gave them four special instructions that believers today would do well to heed.

Please the Lord (Num. 15:1-21). The phrase "to make a sweet savor [aroma] unto the Lord" is found five times in this paragraph (vv. 3, 7, 10, 13-14) and means "an aroma pleasing to the Lord." The five basic Mosaic offerings were the burnt offering, meal offering, peace offering, sin offering, and trespass offering (Lev. 1–7). The first three were "sweet savor" sacrifices, designed to please the Lord, but the sin offering and the trespass offering were not "sweet savor" because they dealt with guilt and sin, and there's nothing pleasing to God about sin.

The burnt offering typified the worshiper's complete devotion to God, for the animal was totally consumed on the altar. The meal (grain) offering spoke of the worshiper's dedication of his labor to the Lord, and the peace (trespass) offering represented joyful fellowship and thanksgiving to God for His blessings.[2]

The sacrifices discussed in these verses were spontaneous expressions of love and gratitude to God. Along with these sacrifices, the worshiper was instructed to offer two quarts of fine flour[3] mixed with about a quart of oil, a portion of which was placed on the altar and the rest given to the priest. The worshiper also brought a quart of wine which the priest poured out at the base of the altar where the blood of the sacrifice was poured out. When larger animals were sacrificed, the amounts of meal, oil, and wine were increased proportionately.

The Jews wouldn't become an agricultural people until they settled in the land, and then they could cultivate vineyards, olive trees, and fields of grain. In adding flour, oil, and wine to the sacrifice, the worshiper was bringing to the Lord the fruits of his labor and the evidence of God's goodness. Today, we bring money as an offering to the Lord, but we wouldn't have that money if He didn't give us jobs and the ability to work (Deut. 8:18).

Christians today see in the fine flour a picture of Jesus Christ, the Bread of Life (John 6), who offered Himself to God for us "as a sweet-smelling aroma" (Eph. 5:2). The flour also acknowledges God as the generous source of all our food. The oil is a symbol of the Holy Spirit (Zech. 4), and the wine reminds us of the joy of the Lord (Ps. 104:15).[4] It pleases the heart of God when His people spontaneously thank Him for the material and spiritual blessings that He sends so faithfully and bountifully.

The drink offering, poured out at the base of the altar, symbolized life poured out for God. On the cross, Jesus "poured out His soul unto death" (Isa. 53:12, NKJV) so that those who trust Him might have eternal life. As we serve the Lord sacrificially, we're like a "drink offering," poured out in the service of others and to the glory of God (Phil. 2:17; 2 Tim. 4:6; and see 2 Sam. 23:14-17).

The resident aliens who lived among the Jews were permitted to bring sweet savor offerings to the Lord (Num. 15:14-16), but nothing is said here about their having to be circumcised (Ex. 12:48). Even the Jewish boys weren't given the mark of the covenant during Israel's years of wandering because the nation had rebelled against God and broken His covenant. The males in the new generation were marked with the covenant sign when they entered the Promised Land (Josh. 5:1-8).

Finally, the women were commanded to give a portion of their dough to the Lord, an offering of firstfruits to acknowledge Him as Lord of their lives (Num. 15:17-21). "Honor the Lord with your possessions, and with the firstfruits of all your increase" (Prov. 3:9). This is the Old Testament version of Matthew 6:33.

Seek the Lord (Num. 15:22-29). The sacrifices described in Leviticus 1–7 took care of sins of commission, but the instructions here have to do with unintentional sins of omission, things that the people should have done but didn't do. The sin might be corporate and involve the entire nation (Num. 15:24-26) or it might be the transgression of an individual (vv. 27-29). Even though the people who sinned didn't realize their failure, what they didn't do was still a sin and had to be dealt with. "I didn't know" will not avail at the throne of God.

The sinners had to come God's appointed way so He could forgive them and restore them to fellowship and blessing. If the whole nation sinned, they had to bring a young bull for a burnt offering (dedication), plus the required drink offering and grain offering, and a male goat for a sin offering (atonement). The individual who sinned had to bring a year-old female goat as a sin offering. God promised to forgive those who truly sought Him by faith (vv. 25-26, 28). Of course, forgiveness didn't come because of the blood of animals, but because Christ shed His blood for sinners, fulfilling what these animals symbolized (Heb. 10:1-18).

Sometimes we sin against the Lord by what we do, and sometimes by what we don't do (Luke 7:36-50). Sins of ignorance aren't automatically forgiven just because we unintentionally forgot God's commands; these sins must be confessed to the Lord just as we confess sins of commission (1 John 1:9).[5] The fact that God forgave sins of omission didn't mean He was "easy on sin," because blood still had to be shed before the sinner could be forgiven.

Fear the Lord (Num. 15:30-36). To sin "presumptuously" means to disobey God's law deliberately and arrogantly, knowing full well the danger involved. The Hebrew literally means "to sin with a high hand" as though the person were shaking his or her fist in the face of God, daring God to do something. Presumptuous sins are committed by people who have "no fear of God before their eyes" (Rom. 3:18).

God commanded that such sinners be cut off from the nation, which means they were stoned to death. Not only had they disobeyed God's Law, but they did it in such a way that they defied God's will and despised God's Word. No sacrifices were provided for deliberate high-handed sins, so there was no forgiveness offered at the altar.[6]

Moses records an example of high-handed sin in the account of the man who gathered fuel on the Sabbath (Num. 15:32-36).

Certainly this man knew God's commandments (Ex. 20:8-11; 31:12-17), and yet he deliberately disobeyed them. Apparently he was gathering sticks to start a fire, and it was unlawful to kindle a fire on the Sabbath (35:1-3). This was a new experience for the Jews, so Moses sought the Lord's will, and God told him to have the people stone the impudent offender to death.

It's a dangerous thing for Christians to say, "I'll go ahead and sin, because afterward, I can ask God to forgive me." They see God's promise in 1 John 1:9 as a "religious rabbit's foot" to get them out of trouble after they've deliberately disobeyed God. Professed Christians who repeatedly and deliberately sin probably aren't Christians at all (Rom. 6; 1 John 3:7-10; 5:1-5, 18); and true believers who adopt that careless attitude will be chastened by the Father until they submit to His will (Heb. 12:3-15). When the German poet Heine said on his deathbed, "Of course God will forgive me; that's His job," he understood neither the awfulness of sin or the high cost of God's grace.

Remember the Lord (Num. 15:37-41). A busy life has its share of demands and distractions, so the Lord gave His people a simple way to remember their obligation to obey His Law. He commanded them to put tassels on the corners of their upper outer garment, with blue thread woven into each tassel. These tassels were reminders that the Jews were God's covenant people and different from the other nations. (See Deut. 22:12; Zech. 8:23; Matt. 23:5.) Modern orthodox Jews have tassels on their prayer shawls.

When they dressed each morning, the Jews would see the tassels and be reminded that they were God's people, obligated to obey His will. Perhaps the blue threads would remind them that their God was in heaven, seeing everything they did. As they walked about during the day, they would notice the tassels and remember God's commandments, and likewise when they prepared for sleep at night. No matter how many idols they might see during the day, the tassels reminded them that it was Jehovah, the God of Israel, who had delivered them from Egypt; and they were to worship and serve Him alone. "Bless the Lord,

O my soul, and forget not all His benefits" (Ps. 103:2).

2. The authority of God's servants (Num. 16:1–17:13)

When you review the history of Israel, from Egypt to Canaan, you discover that the nation got into trouble every time they resisted the leadership of Moses and Aaron. Whenever God sought to build the people's faith by bringing them into a difficult situation, they immediately rebelled against Moses and Aaron, blamed them for their plight, and made plans to return to Egypt.

These chapters record two challenges to the leadership of Moses and Aaron, one from a group of Levites (16:1-35) and one from the people as a whole (vv. 41-50). Out of each of these confrontations came a visible reminder to the Jews of their rebellion: the brass covering on the altar (vv. 36-40) and Aaron's rod that budded (17:1-13).

The first confrontation (Num. 16:1-35). No matter how much God did for them or taught them, Israel was not a spiritually minded people (Deut. 31:16-30). They still had Egypt in their hearts, and their lust for idols stayed with them even while they marched through the wilderness (Amos 5:25-26; Acts 7:42-43). Moses was a godly leader, and Israel could have been a godly people if they had obeyed what he taught them.

1. Korah, a notable leader (Num. 16:1-3). A Levite in the family of Kohath, Korah must have been a distinguished leader to be able to enlist the support of 250 "men of renown" from the other tribes. The fact that the text gives his genealogy is another hint that he was an important man. Numbers 27:3 suggests that men from other tribes were involved in the rebellion, so it was a nationwide conspiracy. The Kohathites carried the tabernacle furniture when Israel marched to a new location, and they camped on the south side of the tabernacle, across from Gad, Simeon, and Reuben. Perhaps this explains how Korah was able to get Dathan, Abiram, and On, three Reubenites, to join him in his crusade.

Whenever you find complaining and rebelling among God's people, there's usually a "stated reason" and a "hidden reason."

Korah's *public* complaint was that Moses and Aaron were "running things" and not giving the people opportunity for input. He wanted more democracy in the camp. After all, the Lord dwelt in the entire camp and all the people were "a kingdom of priests" (Ex. 19:3-6), so who were Moses and Aaron to elevate themselves above everybody else? The *hidden* reason was that Korah wanted the Levites to have the same privileges as Aaron and his sons (Num. 16:10). Korah wasn't satisfied to be assisting the priests; he wanted to be a priest.

Whether it's the ancient camp of Israel or a modern city, no society can function without subordination.[7] Somebody has to be in charge. Parents have authority in the home, teachers in the classroom, managers in the factory or office, and civil servants in the city or nation (Rom. 13; 1 Peter 2:11ff). When this kind of order breaks down, then society is in serious trouble. God had chosen Moses to be leader of the nation and Aaron to be the high priest, and to resist this arrangement was to rebel against the will of God and bring serious division to the camp.

The selfish desire for greatness and authority is a common theme in Scripture, whether it's Korah opposing Moses and Aaron, Absalom defying his father (2 Sam. 15), Adonijah claiming the crown (1 Kings 1), the disciples arguing over which of them was the greatest (Luke 22:44), or Diotrephes loving to have preeminence in a local church (2 John 9-10). And yet the most important place in the Christian life is the place of God's choice, the place He's prepared for us and prepared us to fill. The important thing isn't status but faithfulness, doing the work God wants us to do. Every member of the church, the body of Christ, has a spiritual gift to be used for serving others, and therefore every member is important to God and to the church (1 Cor. 12:14-18).

2. Moses, a humble leader (Num. 16:4-11). As he had done before, Moses fell on his face before the Lord (14:5, 22; 16:22, 45; 20:6; 22:31). He didn't debate with Korah and his crowd and try to change their minds, because he knew their aim was to seize the priesthood, something the Lord would never permit. The Lord would show Korah and his followers how wrong they were, and their pride would ultimately lead to their destruction (Prov. 16:18).

The test Moses proposed was a simple one. If Korah and his men were indeed priests acceptable to God, then let them bring their censers to the tabernacle and see if God would accept them. Surely the rebels remembered what happened to Nadab and Abihu when they rashly brought "strange fire" before the Lord (Lev. 10), but even this warning didn't deter them.

3. Moses, an angry leader (Num. 16:12-17). Moses called Dathan and Abiram to come to the meeting, but they refused. Nothing is said about On, so perhaps he wisely dropped out of the rebellion. The arrogance of these two men is painful to see, for they not only refused to obey Moses, but they blamed him for Israel's sin at Kadesh-Barnea! Even more, they called Egypt a "land of milk and honey" and accused Moses of making himself a prince and "lording it over" the people. Undoubtedly these spiritually ignorant men had envy in their hearts and wanted to take over the leadership themselves.

Again, Moses didn't argue with the rebels; he prayed to the Lord and asked Him to vindicate His servant. Moses' anger wasn't selfish irritation; it was the righteous indignation of a man of integrity who sought only the glory of the Lord. There is a righteous anger that God's people ought to feel when sinners defy the will of God and tempt others to sin (Ex. 32:19; 2 Cor. 11:29; Mark 3:5; Eph. 4:26).

4. Jehovah, the righteous Judge (Num. 16:18-35). The next morning, Korah and his followers showed up with their censers and stood with Moses and Aaron at the entrance of the tabernacle, while Dathan and Abiram stood with their families at the doors of their tents on the south side of the tabernacle. We can imagine the awesome silence that prevailed, and then the glory of the Lord appeared (14:10; 20:6; Ex. 16:10-12) and the voice of the Lord spoke. The hour of God's judgment had arrived!

Moses and Aaron, being true leaders, immediately fell on their faces before the Lord and interceded for the nation. Why should all the people die because of the sin of these men? Moses frequently had to intercede for the people, and they probably didn't appreciate what he did for them. On two occasions, God was ready to destroy the entire nation, but Moses' intercession saved them (Num. 14:10-12; Ex. 32:7-14).

God warned the Jews to move away from the tents of Korah, Dathan, and Abiram; then the earth opened up and swallowed those evil men and their households, and fire from God destroyed the 250 would-be priests (Num. 11:1-3; Lev. 10:1-7).[8] God made it very clear that the Jews were to accept their appointed leaders and respect their authority. It's a dangerous thing for people to challenge God's order and promote themselves to become leaders. They not only rebel against the Lord (Num. 16:11) but against their own lives (v. 38). Dr. A.W. Tozer used to say, "Never follow a leader until you see the anointing oil on his head."

5. *Eleazar the faithful priest (Num. 16:36-40).* Since the 250 censers had been offered to the Lord, they were sanctified, even though the men who held them were wicked, so the censers couldn't be treated like common metal. God ordered Aaron's son Eleazar to gather them up and have them beaten into plates to be put on the altar of burnt offering. These plates would be a lasting reminder to the people that "it is a fearful thing to fall into the hands of the living God" (Heb. 10:31). Whether these plates replaced the original bronze network on which the sacrifices were burned, or were added to it, we aren't told.

When Jude wrote to warn the early church about false teachers, he used Korah as an example, associating him with Cain and Balaam (Jude 11).[9] The word "gainsaying" (KJV; "rebellion," NIV) means "to say against, to oppose in word and deed, to rebel." In his farewell message to the Ephesians elders (Acts 20:28-31), Paul warned about proud people who would seek to seize authority in the local church and promote themselves. It's likely that more churches have been divided because of arrogant leadership than because of false doctrine.

The second confrontation (Num. 16:41–17:13). The deaths of over 250 people should have brought reverent awe into the hearts of the Israelites, but there was "no fear of God before their eyes" (Rom. 3:18). What began with several hundred rebels had now become a national uprising! Instead of falling to their knees and crying out to God for forgiveness and mercy, the Jews were rebelling against Moses and Aaron just as Korah had done! Carnally minded people can't perceive the spiritual meaning of what God does because they lack spiritual discernment (1 Cor. 2). The nation beheld God's acts, but Moses understood God's ways (Ps. 103:7).

Again, the glory of the Lord appeared and the judgment of the Lord began to consume the Israelites; for the second time in two days, Moses and Aaron fell on their faces and interceded for the people. Aaron took a censer and ran into the ranks of people who were already smitten, and he "stood between the dead and the living, and the plague was stayed" (Num. 16:48). When they counted the corpses, they found that 14,700 people had died because of their foolish rebellion against the Lord. "The wages of sin is death" (Rom. 6:23).

What is there about the human heart that makes it so easy to follow the crowd and disobey the Lord? "But what experience and history teach us is this, that peoples and governments have never learned anything from history, or acted on principles deduced from it." So wrote the German philosopher Hegel in the introduction to his *Philosophy of History*, and he was right. The one thing we learn from history is that we don't learn from history, and that includes church history.

1. A second reminder (17:1-13). God would prove once and for all that He had chosen Aaron and his sons to serve as priests, and that any attempts on the part of any other tribe to seize the priesthood would meet with the wrath of God.

The test was a simple one. The leader of each tribe gave Moses a rod (staff) bearing the tribal name, and all twelve rods plus Aaron's rod were put before the Lord in the holy of holies. The fact that all the tribes were included in the test suggests that all of them had been represented in the insurrection. The rod that sprouted would belong to the man God had chosen to be the nation's priest. When Moses brought out the rods the next day, everybody could see that only Aaron's rod had produced life. Aaron's staff "had not only sprouted but had budded, blossomed and produced almonds" (v. 8, NIV). What more evidence could the Israelites want?

If Moses put Aaron's rod back into the holy of holies, how could it be a reminder to the nation that the tribe of Levi was the priestly tribe? For one thing, the rulers of each tribe and many of the people saw the rods and could bear witness that Aaron's was the only one that produced life. Each day, when the tribal leaders took up their staffs, they would be reminded that God had chosen Aaron's sons to serve at the altar. Furthermore, the high priest could always bring out the staff of Levi as unchanging evidence that Aaron's family alone was chosen for the priesthood.

As usual, the Israelites overreacted when they heard the news and concluded that anybody who came near the tabernacle would perish (vv. 12-13; see 14:40-45). At least they had a fear of judgment, but they didn't have a true fear of God in their hearts. But the presence of the tabernacle in the camp should have been a source of confidence for the Jews, for it meant that Jehovah was present with them. He would guide them through the wilderness, defeat their enemies, receive their sacrifices, and grant them forgiveness. To calm their fears, Moses in the next two chapters explained the ministry of the priests and the importance of the tabernacle of the camp.

The Lord gave Israel three reminders to encourage them to obey His Law and submit to His will: the tassels on their garments, the brass plates on the altar, and Aaron's rod in the holy of holies. To encourage believers today to be obedient children, the Lord has given us His Word (John 17:17), the indwelling Holy Spirit (1 Cor. 6:19-20), the Lord's Supper, reminding us of the death of Christ and His promised return (11:23-34; 1 John 3:1-3), and the interceding Savior in heaven (Heb. 4:14-16; Rom. 8:34). Before we judge God's ancient people, perhaps we'd better examine our own hearts to see if we've submitted to the authority of His Word and of His appointed leaders.

SEVEN

Another Crisis at Kadesh

It's probable that the instructions in chapters 18 and 19 were given by the Lord while Israel was still at Kadesh-Barnea. However, when you get to chapter 20, the nation has completed its thirty-eight years of wandering and is back at Kadesh (20:1, 16).

Very little is written in Numbers about Israel's years of wandering, although a list of their camping places in found in Numbers 33. Miriam died in the first month of the fortieth year (20:1), when the nation had returned to Kadesh; and Aaron died in the fifth month of that same year (33:38). When Moses died at the end of the fortieth year (Deut. 1:3), the entire older generation had perished, except for Joshua and Caleb, who were permitted to enter Canaan.

God's people had been stubborn and rebellious, and the Lord had chastened them for it, but in spite of their disobedience, the Lord had been faithful to care for them. "Nevertheless, He saved them for His name's sake, that He might make His mighty power to be known" (Ps. 106:8). Consider some of the Lord's concerns on behalf of His people as expressed by the instructions and events found in these chapters.

1. Guarding the sanctuary (Num. 18:1-7)

Because of the Lord's judgments against the rebels at the tabernacle (16:31-35) and His miraculous defense of Aaron's high priestly ministry (17:10-13), the people of Israel were terrified even to have the tabernacle in their camp. "Are we all going to die?" they cried (17:13, NIV). Actually, God's presence in their camp was the distinctive mark of the people of Israel (Ex. 33:1-16), for Israel was the only nation to have the glory of the living God present with them and going before them (Rom. 9:4).

God spoke expressly to Aaron (Num. 18:1, 8, 20) and thereby elevated his high priestly ministry even more. The Lord made it clear that it was the responsibility of the priests to minister in the tabernacle and protect it from defilement, and it was the responsibility of the Levites to assist the priests in their tabernacle ministry.[1] As long as the priests and Levites obeyed this rule, there would be no judgment sent to the people (v. 5).

The priestly ministry was a serious matter, for if the priests didn't follow God's instructions, they might die. If they permitted an unauthorized person to come near the tabernacle or to minister there, God could slay them. It was dangerous to disobey even in the matter of how they dressed (Ex. 28:35, 42-43) or if they washed regularly (30:17-21). God held Aaron and his sons responsible for offenses committed against the sanctuary and the priesthood.

The priesthood was God's gift to Israel, for without priests the people couldn't approach God. The Levites were God's gift to the priests, relieving them of menial tasks so they could devote themselves fully to serving God and the people. The seven men appointed in Acts 6, usually called deacons, had a similar relationship to the apostles. There's nothing demeaning about serving tables, but the apostles had more important work to do.

Everything rises or falls with leadership, and Aaron was the leader of the priestly family. He was accountable to God for what happened at the sanctuary. God doesn't dwell in temples made with hands (Acts 7:48), but He does dwell in our bodies by His Holy Spirit (1 Cor. 6:19-20) and among His people in the local assembly (3:16ff). We must be careful how we treat our bodies and what we do to the church of Jesus Christ. "If anyone destroys God's temple, God will destroy him; for God's temple is sacred, and you are that temple" (v. 17, NIV).

2. Caring for His servants (Num. 18:8-32)

As servants of God, the priests and Levites deserved to be cared for by the people of God. Unlike the other tribes, Levi would have no inheritance in the Promised Land, for the Lord was their inheritance (v. 20; Deut. 10:8-9; Josh. 13:14, 33; 14:13; 18:7), and the Levites would be given forty-eight towns to live in (Num. 35:1-8; Josh. 21).[2] Both the priests and Levites were cared for by means of the sacrifices, offerings, and tithes of the people.

The priests (Num. 18:8-20). God assigned to the priests portions of the meal offerings, sin offerings, trespass offerings, and peace offerings (Lev. 6:14–7:38), as well as the firstfruits (Deut. 26:1-11) and the firstborn animals that the people brought to the Lord. Some of this food only the priests could eat, but much of it could be shared with their families. However, whoever in the priestly family ate of the sacrifices given to God had to be ceremonially clean and treat the food with reverence, because it had been sanctified by being presented to God.

The Levites (Num. 18:21-32). They were given the tithes which the people brought to God's sanctuary, for 10 percent of the produce belonged to the Lord. The Jews were obligated to pay three different tithes: a tithe to the Levites (vv. 21-24), a tithe "eaten before the Lord" (Deut. 14:22-27), and a tithe every three years that was given to the poor (Lev. 27:28-29). The Levites in turn were to take a tithe of what they received, offer it to the Lord, and give it to the high priest.

The principle here is clear and is emphasized often in Scripture: Those who serve the Lord and His people should be supported from the material blessings God gives His people. "The laborer is worthy of his hire" (Luke 10:7; Matt. 10:10), said Jesus; and Paul wrote, "Even so the Lord has commanded that those who preach the Gospel should live from the Gospel" (1 Cor.

3:14, NKJV). Paul further explained this principle in Galatians 6:6-10; Philippians 4:10-19; and 1 Timothy 5:17-18.

The Jewish people didn't always obey this law and bring their tithes to the Lord, and as a consequence the ministry at the tabernacle and temple suffered. (See Neh. 10:35-39; 12:44-47; 13:10-14; Mal. 1:6–2:9.) If the priests and Levites didn't have food for their families, then they had to leave the sanctuary and go to work in the fields (Neh. 13:10). It's tragic when God's people don't love the Lord and the Lord's house enough to support it faithfully.

God expected the Levites to tithe what they received and share it with the high priest (Num. 18:25-32). On occasion I've met people in Christian service who don't give to the Lord's work because they consider themselves exempt. "We're serving the Lord and all that we have belongs to Him," they argue, but their argument doesn't hold water. The Levites were serving God full time, yet they tithed what they received.

Tithing isn't necessarily a legalistic practice, for Abraham and Jacob tithed centuries before the Law was given (Gen. 14:20; 28:22). If the Jews under the Old Covenant could give 10 percent of their income (produce) to the Lord, can Christians under the New Covenant do less? For us, tithing is just the beginning! If we grasp the meaning of 2 Corinthians 8–9, we'll practice "grace giving" and go far beyond the tithe.[3]

3. Cleansing the defiled (Num. 19:1-22)

In their daily lives, the Jewish people had to be sensitive to what was "clean" and what was "unclean," for this determined their relationship to the Lord and the other people in the camp. God's rule was, "You shall be holy for I am holy," a statement found eight times in the Bible (Lev. 11:44-45; 19:2; 20:7, 26; 21:8; 1 Peter 1:15-16). The regulations about "clean and unclean" are spelled out in detail in Leviticus 11–15, telling the Israelites what they could eat, how they should deal with bodily discharges and infections, and what to do about dead bodies. Certainly there was a hygienic purpose behind these laws, but there was also a spiritual purpose: to teach the Jews the difference between holiness and sin and encourage them to walk in holiness.

The preparation (Num. 19:1-10). There are several unique features about this ritual. The animal chosen was not male; it was slain outside the camp, away from the tabernacle and the altar; it was slain by a layman and not a priest; the blood was not caught and poured out before God but burned with the carcass; and the ashes were gathered to be mixed with water and used for ceremonial purification.

First, the animal that was selected had to be without blemish, red in color, and never yoked for service. The red color may point to the blood being shed, but perhaps the color speaks of the red earth out of which the first man was made (Gen. 2:7). The name "Adam" comes from the Hebrew word *adamah* which means "red earth."

Aaron's son and successor Eleazar led the heifer outside the camp where a layman killed it in the presence of the priest. The word used for the slaughtering of the animal is not the word used for sacrificing an animal, and there is no altar involved. Eleazar caught some of the blood and sprinkled it toward the tabernacle seven times.

The carcass with the blood was then burned, and the word used here is not the normal word for "the burning of a sacrifice." While the body was burning, Eleazar dropped three important items into the fire: cedar wood, hyssop (a porous plant that absorbs liquid), and scarlet wool, all of which were used in the cleansing ceremony for a healed leper (Lev. 14:4, 6, 49, 51-52; and see Ps. 51:7).

Because of their involvement with a dead body, Eleazar and the man assisting him were considered ceremonially unclean and had to wash themselves and their clothing before returning to the camp in the evening. A man ceremonially clean gathered up the ashes into a container and placed it in a clean place outside the camp, accessible to the people. He too had to wash before he could return to the camp.

The application (Num. 19:11-22). How were these ashes used?

People who became ceremonially defiled from touching a dead body (vv. 11-13), being in a tent where somebody died (vv. 14-15), or touching anything that itself was defiled (v. 16), could be made clean again by using the ashes. They would have to wait three days after their defilement and then go out of the camp with a ceremonially clean man to the place where the ashes were kept. The man would mix some of the ashes with running water in a vessel, dip hyssop into the water and sprinkle it on the unclean person. This would be repeated four days later on the seventh day. The cleansed persons would then wash themselves and their clothes and wait until evening to return to the camp.

It was a very serious offense if a defiled person refused to be purified, because defiled people defiled the camp. God's presence dwelt in the tabernacle (vv. 13, 20) and He walked among the people (Lev. 26:11-12; Deut. 23:12-14); therefore, the camp had to be kept holy. Unclean people who refused to be cleansed were cut off from the nation (Num. 19:20) and stoned to death.

The church today doesn't worry about external ritual un-cleanness, but we should take to heart the lesson of this chapter that God wants us to be a holy people. We should "cleanse our-selves of all filthiness of the flesh and of the spirit, perfecting holiness in the fear of God" (2 Cor. 7:1). God promises forgive-ness and cleansing to His children if they turn from their sins and confess them to the Lord (1 John 1:9). An innocent animal had to die to provide ritual cleansing for the Jews, but the innocent Lamb of God had to die to provide cleansing for us (John 1:29; 1 Peter 1:18-23).

4. Chastening His leaders (Num. 20:1-13)

The death of Miriam must have affected Moses and Aaron deeply. It was Miriam whom the Lord used to save Moses' life when he was a baby, and she even arranged for their own mother to raise Moses and be paid for it (Ex. 2). She had led the praises of the women at the Red Sea (Ex. 15) and had endured the wilderness trials with her brothers. The only blemish on the record is her criticism of Moses (Num. 12), but is there any servant of God who has a spotless page?

An old problem (Num. 20:1-5). It was a conditioned reflex: whenever the Israelites faced a difficulty, they complained about it to Moses and Aaron and wept because they hadn't stayed in Egypt. Difficulties either bring out the best in people or the worst; they either mature us or make us more childish (James 1:2-8). Israel's words and attitudes revealed clearly that their hearts were still in Egypt. What a picture of the professed Christian who still loves the world (1 John 2:15-17) and turns to the world for help whenever there's a problem!

A divine solution (Num. 20:6-9). It was the people who should have been on their faces, confessing their sins and seeking God's forgiveness, but once again, Moses and Aaron fell before the Lord and sought His wisdom and help (14:5; 16:4, 22, 45; 22:31). Spiritual leaders pay a price as they seek to serve God's people, but the people usually don't appreciate it. The same people repeat the same sins and refuse to trust God and obey Him.

The rod was the same one Moses had used to do wonders in Egypt, especially to open the Red Sea. The Hebrew word for "rock" means a high cliff, a place for a fortress, and not a boulder. God is able to solve our problems no matter what the circumstances are, provided we trust Him and do His will.

An impulsive sin (Num. 20:10-11). Provoked in his spirit, instead of speaking to the rock, Moses smote it twice. He also spoke angrily to the people, calling them "rebels," and he gave the impression that he and Aaron had supplied the water. It was a sad demonstration of hostility by the meekest man on the earth (12:3), showing that we can fail in our strengths as well as our weaknesses.[4]

Moses was human, just as we are, and was no doubt weary as he drew near to the end of the wilderness march, during which he'd seen nothing but unbelief and heard nothing but complaining. Psalm 106:32-33 states that it was the people who provoked Moses to anger, and that isn't hard to believe. Perhaps he was emotionally drained because of the death of his sister. He may have been upset because, when the people complained, the Lord didn't reveal His glory and judgment as He had done before.

But no matter what mitigating causes we might produce, the fact still remains that Moses didn't honor the Lord or obey His orders. By striking the rock, he ruined a type of the Messiah who gives living water to His people (Ex. 17:1-7; John 7:37-39). Our Lord gave Himself for us on the cross only once and doesn't have to be crucified (smitten) again (Heb. 9:26-28). Now all that believers need do is ask, and God gives His Spirit to them.

The remarkable thing is that God gave the water, even though Moses' attitudes and actions were all wrong![5] "He has not dealt with us according to our sins, nor punished us according to our iniquities" (Ps. 103:10, NKJV). "If You, Lord, should mark iniquities, O Lord, who could stand?" (Ps. 130:3, NKJV) God in His grace met the needs of His people because He is a God of compassion and infinite goodness, but He did not overlook Moses' sins.

A painful discipline (Num. 20:12-13). The people were helped but Moses was disciplined, and in a most painful way: He wasn't permitted to enter the Promised Land (Luke 12:48). He had glorified himself instead of glorifying God. Once again, an important Old Testament type is involved, for the Law (Moses) cannot give us our inheritance (Gal. 3:18). Joshua is a type of Jesus Christ the conqueror, and only he could lead the people into their promised inheritance (Heb. 4:1-11). Had Moses entered the land with the people, he would have ruined the message of the Book of Hebrews![6]

The first time God provided water for Israel, Moses called the place "Massah and Meribah" which means "testing and quarreling." On this second occasion, Moses called the place "Meribah" ("quarreling"), but it was he who had been tested, and he failed the test. At one point, Moses begged God to let him go over the Jordan, but the Lord refused his request (Deut. 3:23-29). Moses revealed his meekness by submitting to God's discipline and continuing to lead the people.

5. Guiding His people (Num. 20:14-22)
Israel was now marching north to the Plains of Moab (33:48)

where Moses would prepare the new generation to enter the land. The easiest route was through Edom on the king's highway, the main trade route at that time. The Edomites were the descendants of Esau (Gen. 36) and therefore related to Israel, for Jacob was Esau's brother.

Knowing the history of conflict between Esau and Jacob, Moses used sound diplomatic tactics as he requested permission to pass through the land. Israel had conquered many kings and nations during their march, and the Edomites knew this, so Moses had to make it clear that this was a peaceful march. We get the impression that Numbers 20:14-17 was originally a written document taken to the king of Edom by ambassadors from Israel. While a prince in Egypt, Moses would have learned all about these diplomatic matters.

First, Moses emphasized the fact that the Jews and Edomites were brothers (v. 14), and twice he used the phrase "our fathers" (v. 15). This common heritage should have caused the Edomite leaders to have some sympathy for their brothers. Then Moses reminded the Edomites of Israel's suffering and bondage in Egypt and the miraculous deliverance the Lord gave them. Since God delivered them and was directing them, surely the Edomites would want to cooperate with Jehovah and let their Jewish relatives march through the land.

But to have between 2 and 3 million people and their livestock go through your land could be a costly thing, because they would need food and water. Directed by the Lord (Deut. 2:1-8), Moses assured the people of Edom that his people would pay for their food and water and not even enter the fields or vineyards of Edom. Moses was making every effort to guarantee a peaceful journey, but the Edomites refused to accept his generous offer. Moses tried a second time to persuade the Edomites, but his words only provoked more opposition.

Jacob and Esau had met and settled their differences years before (Gen. 32–33), but Esau's descendants were perpetuating the old family feud. Years later, when Jerusalem was attacked, the Edomites assisted the enemy and even stopped the Jewish fugitives from escaping (the Book of Obadiah; Ps. 137:7). It's tragic when a family feud is kept alive from generation to generation, poisoning hearts and minds and keeping brothers from helping one another.

When the Edomite army arrived and stood in the way, it was obvious that the wisest course for Israel was to choose a new route. Certainly God could have helped Israel destroy the entire Edomite army, but that wasn't His plan. "If it is possible, as much as depends on you, live peaceably with all men" (Rom. 12:18, NKJV). God would take care of Edom when the time came (see Obadiah); meanwhile, Israel took an alternative route and arrived at Mount Hor. We don't know the location of Mount Hor, but that was where Aaron died and was buried.

6. Perpetuating the priesthood (Num. 20:23-29)
Both Moses and Aaron had rebelled against God when Moses smote the rock, so neither of them would enter the Promised Land. On the first day of the fifth month of that fortieth year (33:38), Moses, Aaron, and Eleazar went somewhere on Mount Hor because it was now time for Aaron to die. Moses would say good-bye to a beloved brother and Eleazar to a revered father. Aaron was 123 years old (33:38-39).

However, Aaron's death didn't interrupt the ministry of the priesthood, for Eleazar took his place. As John Wesley used to say, "God buries His workmen but His work goes on." In fulfillment of the Law (Ex. 29:29-30), Moses took the holy garments from his brother, Aaron, and put them on Eleazar. He probably anointed him as well for the new office. When Moses and Eleazar returned to the camp without Aaron, and the people saw Eleazar dressed in the robes of the high priest, they knew that Aaron's life had ended. They mourned for Aaron for thirty days, which takes us now into the sixth month.

Eleazar was the third son of Aaron (Num. 3:2); the first two, Nadab and Abihu, were slain by the Lord for defiling the tabernacle with false fire (Lev. 10). Before becoming high priest, he was the chief leader of the Levites for caring for the tabernacle (Num. 3:32; 4:16). He would assist Moses in taking the census of the new generation (26:1-3) as well as in commissioning Joshua to succeed Moses (27:18-23). When Israel had conquered the land, Eleazar helped Joshua assign each tribe its inheritance (34:17; Josh. 14:1; 19:15).

Moses has experienced two family funerals, two confrontations with critics in the camp, and a personal failure at Kadesh; yet he picks up his rod and goes right back to work. Victorious Christian service, like the victorious Christian life, is a series of new beginnings. No matter what mistakes we've made, it's always too soon to quit.

EIGHT

Marching in Victory—and Defeat

It's remarkable how many unconverted people have the mistaken idea that the Christian life is boring. How can walking with God be boring when our Father in heaven arranges the experiences of life for our good and His glory? For the Christian believer, life becomes a school (Ps. 90:12) in which we learn more about God and His Word, as well as more about ourselves and how much we need to grow. Life also becomes a gymnasium and a battlefield (Heb. 12; 2 Tim. 2:1-5) where we must exercise our faith and develop strong spiritual muscles for running the race and fighting the battle.

This truth is well illustrated in Numbers 21, a chapter in which God's care and discipline of His people are so evident.

1. The power of God (Num. 21:1-3)

Life goes on. The Jews completed their mourning for Aaron and were soon back on the road and back in the battle. Arad was a Canaanite town about twenty miles south of Hebron, so the new generation of Israelites was facing its first conflict with the Canaanites. The Jewish army would spend at least seven years conquering the nations in the Promised Land, so God gave them some military training as they marched on the road to Atharim.[1]

The news of Israel's march from Egypt to Kadesh had gone before them and the rulers of the city-states in and around Canaan weren't going to give in to these intruders without a fight. Apparently Israel wasn't prepared for this first attack because some of their people were taken prisoners, but the leaders immediately turned to the Lord for His help. They vowed to utterly destroy the Canaanites and their cities if the Lord would give them victory.

To "utterly destroy" meant to devote something completely to the Lord (Lev. 27:28-29; Deut. 7:2-6), wiping out the people and their cities and giving all the spoils to God. This is what Israel would do at Jericho (Josh. 6:17-21), and because Achan took what belonged to God, he was slain (Josh. 7).[2] The Canaanite culture was unspeakably wicked, especially their religious practices, and God wanted these nations removed from the earth.

God gave Israel victory over the enemy and the people kept their promise. They destroyed Arad and the other cities connected with it and gave a new name to the area: Hormah, which means "destruction." This conflict was quite a contrast to the defeat Israel experienced thirty-eight years before when they tried to engage the enemy without the blessing of God (Num. 14:39-45). When Joshua assigned the tribes their inheritance in Canaan, he gave this area to Judah (Josh. 15:30) and Simeon (19:1, 4).

2. The grace of God (Num. 21:4-9)

This first victory certainly encouraged the Israelites, but it's one thing to "mount up with wings like eagles" and quite something else to "walk and not faint" (Isa. 40:31). Courage in the battle must be followed by endurance in the race. Because the Edomites wouldn't give Israel right-of-way through their land, Moses had to lead the people east of Edom and then north through difficult terrain. It didn't take long before the difficulty of the march made the people impatient, and they started complaining again. It's easy for us to win the battle but lose the victory!

Their sin (Num. 21:5). The anger and impatience in their hearts boiled over into harsh words against the Lord and against Moses. In both their attitudes and their words, they were tempting the Lord (1 Cor. 10:9), and that was a dangerous thing to do. It was the same old complaint: Moses had brought them out of Egypt to die in the wilderness, and there was nothing to eat but manna. In the difficulties of the daily march, they'd forgotten God's promise that they would enter the Promised Land and claim it as their home (Num. 15:1). A bountiful supply of manna had been sent from heaven each morning since shortly after the Exodus (Ex. 16:1-22), so for forty years, God had been feeding His people the nourishment they needed. Manna was "angels' food" (Ps. 78:25), but the people had gotten so accustomed to their blessings that they detested it and called it "this good-for-nothing bread." (See Num. 11:4-6.)

According to John 6, the manna was much more than daily food for Israel: it was a type of Jesus Christ, the Son of God, the "Bread of Life" (vv. 32-40). The manna came only to Israel, but Jesus came to be the Savior of the world. All the manna could do was sustain life, but Jesus Christ *gives* life. When the Jews despised the manna, they were actually rejecting the Son of God. Once more, God had tested His people, and they had failed the test (Deut. 8:15-16).

The Word of God is the "bread of heaven" that God's people must feed on daily if they're going to succeed in their pilgrim journey (Matt. 4:4). The way we treat His Word at the beginning of each day reveals whether or not we are yielded to Him and want to obey Him. To enter a new day without first feeding on the heavenly manna is to invite disappointment and defeat.

Their punishment (Num. 21:6). In the past, when Israel had sinned, the glory of the Lord would usually appear and the judgment of the Lord would follow. But this time, there was no warning. The judgment came immediately as the Lord sent poisonous snakes among the people. They had rejected God's gift of life and health from heaven, so God sent them suffering and death from the earth, and many of the people died.

The word "fiery" is the translation of the Hebrew word *saraph* which means "burning" and also refers to the angelic creatures (seraphim) who minister before the holy throne of God (Isa. 6:2, 6). "Fiery" doesn't describe the appearance of the serpents but the inflammation and pain caused by their venom. Those bitten died quickly and apparently their death wasn't an easy one. The wages of sin is still death.

Their confession and plea (Num. 21:7). Israel had complained and rebelled many times, and once before had admitted, "We have sinned" (14:40), but this is the first time their "We have sinned" seems to be sincere.[3] In the past, Moses had fallen on his face before the Lord and interceded for the people, but now the people begged him to pray for them. Did this mean that the new generation had a more sensitive heart toward the Lord? We hope so.

Their deliverance (Num. 21:8-9). Moses did pray for the people, but the Lord didn't answer in the way the people might have expected. Instead of immediately removing the serpents and healing the people who had been bitten, God instructed Moses to make a serpent of brass and put it on a pole where all the people could see it. If those who had been bitten looked at the serpent, they would be instantly healed.

Jesus used the bronze serpent to illustrate His own death on the cross (John 3:14). ("Lifted up" was a phrase used in that day to refer to crucifixion.) The comparisons between the bronze serpent in Moses' day and the Cross of Christ help us better understand the meaning of God's grace in salvation. All people have been infected by sin and will one day die and face judgment (Heb. 9:27), but if they look by faith to Christ, He will save them and give them eternal life. Looking to the bronze serpent saved people from physical death, but looking to Christ saves us from eternal death.

But why should Moses make a model of *a serpent*, the very creature that was causing the people to die? Because on the cross, Jesus became sin for us—the very thing that condemns people—and bore in His body that which brings spiritual death (2 Cor.

5:21; Rom. 8:3; Gal. 3:13; 1 Peter 2:22-24). Moses didn't hide the bronze serpent; he lifted it up on a pole and put the pole where everybody could see it! So our Lord was crucified publicly, outside the city of Jerusalem, and those who hear the Gospel can "look to Him" and be saved. "For whosoever shall call upon the name of the Lord shall be saved" (Rom. 10:13).

Moses didn't stick the pole inside the tabernacle or even in the tabernacle court, because nobody is saved by keeping the Law. The uplifted serpent was the only cure in the camp, just as Jesus Christ is the only Savior of sinners in the world (Acts 4:12; John 14:6). Nobody could look at the bronze serpent for another person; each dying sinner had to look for himself or herself. The salvation Christ offers is personal and individual, and each of us must look to Christ by faith. No matter how hard they tried, no dying Jew could save himself or herself. The only salvation available was what God had graciously provided, and if you rejected it, you died.

Sin and death came into this world through a look (Gen. 3:6), and the only deliverance from sin and eternal death is by a look of faith: "Look to Me, and be saved, all you ends of the earth" (Isa. 45:22, NKJV). To look means to exercise faith, and the only way to be saved is by faith (Eph. 2:8-19). A dying Jew might argue, "It's a foolish remedy," but it still worked (1 Cor. 1:18-25). Or the dying Israelite might say, "It's too simple," but the remedy still worked.

Imagine the joy in the camp of Israel when the word got out that there was a cure available for everybody! The only people who couldn't be delivered from death were those who for some reason wouldn't look by faith, *or those who didn't know that a remedy was available*. How important it is for us to get the good news out that "Christ Jesus came into the world to save sinners" (1 Tim. 1:15).

3. The goodness of God (Num. 21:10-20)
Leaving the field of battle, Israel continued to march north, crossing the Zared River and camping there. Then they crossed

the Arnon River and approached the country of the Amorites, traveling between Moabite and Amorite country. In Numbers 22–24, we'll meet the Moabites again and see how they tricked Israel into disobeying God.

In 21:14-15, we have a description of the area, taken from an ancient record called *The Book of the Wars of the Lord*. This lost book was apparently a compendium of detailed information about the travels and the battles of Israel.[4] Here it is quoted to describe the geography of the area through which Israel was then passing. It was not comfortable terrain, but the Lord gave His people the strength they needed to make the journey.

When they arrived at Beer ("well"), the Lord anticipated the nation's need and promised to give them water. (See Ex. 17:1-7; Num. 20:2-13; 21:6.) "What shall we eat?" and "What shall we drink?" seemed to be the major concerns of the people (Matt. 6:24-34), just as they are the major concerns of people today, along with "What shall we wear?" But on this occasion, the people didn't complain. Instead, they sang a song! As far as the record is concerned, this is the first time we find Israel singing since God delivered them from Egypt forty years before (Ex. 15).

"The Song of the Well" (Num. 21:16-18) celebrated the Lord's provision of water for the people in the wilderness. It's not likely that the leaders of Israel actually dug the well scepters with their staffs (NIV), because in the sandy wasteland they would have needed much better tools. Since this is a song, we must leave room for poetic expression. What may have happened is that God showed Moses where the water was located, the leaders all thrust their staffs into the ground around that place, and the well opened up and the water gushed out.

The people rejoiced that God gave them the necessities of life, and they found joy in praising Him for His goodness. Water was a precious commodity in the wilderness and the Jews didn't take it for granted, the way too many people today take natural resources for granted, waste them, and pollute them. When God the Creator is left out of the picture, then men and women cease to see themselves as stewards and behave only as selfish consumers. One day God will destroy those who destroy the earth (Rev. 11:18).

This is a good place to pause and note the pictures of our Lord Jesus Christ that are found in the narrative so far. We've seen Him in the manna as the Bread of Life (John 6), and now in the well He's the giver of the living water (7:37-39). In the Bible, water for drinking is a picture of the Spirit of God, while water for washing is a type of the Word of God (Eph. 5:26-27). But before Jesus could send the Spirit, He had to die on the cross (John 7:39), which leads us to the uplifted serpent in Numbers 21:4-9 and John 3:14. The manna emphasizes His incarnation,[5] the serpent His crucifixion, and the water His ascension and the outpouring of the Spirit.

3. The victory of God (Num. 21:21-35)

Before they arrived at the plains of Moab, the Israelites fought two major battles and with the help of the Lord won both of them.

Victory over the Amorites (Num. 21:21-32). As the Jews continued their journey, they arrived at the country of the Amorites. They were descendants of Noah's son Ham through his son Canaan (Gen. 10:6-15) and should not be confused with the Ammonites. God prohibited Israel from confronting the Ammonites (Deut. 2:18-19) because they were related to the Jews through Lot, Abraham's nephew (Gen. 19:30-38).

At one time the Amorites ruled vast areas in Mesopotamia and Syria, but in Moses' day, their territory was much smaller. The Amorites were located on the western shore of the Dead Sea, north of the Edomites, between the Arnon and Jabbock Rivers. In God's eyes, they were a wicked people, ripe for judgment (15:16), and Moses knew that the Lord had promised Israel victory over this evil nation (Ex. 23:23). However, Moses first tried diplomacy, as he had done with the Edomites (Num. 20:14-22), assuring Sihon the king of Heshbon that Israel had come in peace and would create no problems (Deut. 2:26-37).

The Lord wanted Israel to possess the land east of the Jordan, so He permitted Sihon to attack Israel. Sihon's capital was at Heshbon, but he and his army came south to Jahaz, about twenty miles north of the Arnon River, and there challenged Israel. God's people won the battle and possessed the land from the Arnon to the Jabbock River. Before Israel entered the Promised Land, the territory east of the Jordan River was given to Reuben, Gad, and Manasseh (Num. 32).

In Numbers 21:27-30, Moses quoted an Amorite "war song" and applied it to the people of Israel. The song originally celebrated a great Amorite victory when Sihon defeated Moab and took their cities and their people captive. But now it's Sihon and the Amorites who are the losers. Sihon had defeated Chemosh, the god of the Moabites; but Jehovah had defeated the gods of the Amorites! The first six lines of the song (vv. 27-28) describe Sihon's victory over Moab, but the last two lines (v. 30) describe Israel's victory over Sihon.[6]

In writing the Book of Numbers, Moses was led by the Holy Spirit to record this song and apply it to Israel. In fact, the Prophet Jeremiah also quoted part of this song in his prophecy concerning the judgment of Moab (Jer. 48:45-46). Does this mean that God's people today can borrow "secular songs" and use them in worshiping God? No, it doesn't, for Israel used this "taunt song" on the battlefield, not in the sanctuary. Moses was writing history, not liturgy, and Jeremiah was writing prophecy.[7] Christian lyricists have borrowed secular tunes,[8] but we're on dangerous ground when we borrow secular words to express our praise and worship to God.

Victory over Bashan (Num. 21:33-35). After a "mop-up" operation around Jazer, Israel turned its attention to Bashan, a very fertile region east of the Sea of Galilee and south of Mount Hermon. During Abraham's time, a people called the Rephaites lived there (Gen. 14:5). Og, king of Bashan, confronted Israel at Edrei, a town about fifty miles northeast of Jazer, but the Lord assured Moses that Israel would win the victory, and they did.

According to Joshua 2:10, the news of this victory spread to Jericho and brought fear to the hearts of the inhabitants. Ezra mentioned this victory in his prayer (Neh. 9:22) and the psalmists in their songs of praise (Pss. 135:11; 136:19-20). Og had his capital in Ashtaroth (Deut. 1:4) and ruled over sixty cities (Josh. 13:30), all of which Israel captured and destroyed, leaving no survivors (Num. 21:35; Deut. 3:1-11).

In their conquest of Canaan, Israel followed the pattern described in Numbers 21:32-35. Joshua would send out spies to get the lay of the land. Then he would seek God's special instructions for each attack, obey God's orders by faith, and win the victory. The two times that Joshua didn't follow this pattern, he was defeated (Josh. 7 and 9).

The entire region east of the Jordan River was now in the hands of the Israelites and was eventually turned over to the tribes of Reuben, Gad, and Manasseh (Num. 21:32; Deut. 29:7-8). However, Israel would now confront the Moabites who would adopt a subtle strategy that would bring death to 24,000 Jews.

INTERLUDE

The story of Balaam, the mysterious soothsayer, is given in Numbers 22–25. Because this is a complete unit, we will follow the suggested outline given below. Chapter 9 will cover Numbers 22:1–23:26, and chapter 10 will cover Numbers 23:27–25:18.

1. Balaam and God's will (22:1-35)
    (1) The king's request—(22:1-20)
    (2) The donkey's resistance—(22:21-30)
    (3) The angel's revelation—(22:31-35)

2. Balaam and God's message (22:36–24:25)
    (1) The first oracle—(22:26–23:12) a separated people
    (2) The second oracle—(23:13-26) a conquering people
    (3) The third oracle—(23:27–24:14) a prosperous people
    (4) The fourth oracle—(24:15-19) a royal people
    (5) Three concluding oracles—(24:20-25)

3. Balaam and God's people (25:1-18)
    (1) The sin of Israel—(25:1-9)
    (2) The courage of Phinehas—(25:10-15)
    (3) The judgment of Midian—(25:16-18)

4. Balaam and the church today
    (1) The way of Balaam—(2 Peter 2:15)
    (2) The error of Balaam—(Jude 11)
    (3) The doctrine of Balaam—(Rev. 2:14)

Before studying the details, you may want to read Numbers 22–25 at one sitting in order to get the overall picture. Note also the three important New Testament references in Part 4 of the outline, as well as the following Old Testament references: Numbers 31:8; Deuteronomy 4:3-4; 23:3-6; Joshua 13:22; 24:9-10; Nehemiah 13:1-3.

NINE

Principalities and Powers—Part I

On Passover night, the people of Israel marched out of Egypt like conquering soldiers, and God buried the pursuing Egyptian army under the waters of the Red Sea. Except for the Canaanites that Israel rashly attacked out of the will of God (14:39-45), every enemy Israel encountered, they defeated: Amalek (Ex. 17:8-16), the king of Arad (Num. 21:1-3), the Amorites (vv. 21-25) and the forces of Og, king of Bashan (vv. 33-35).

But when Israel arrived on the plains of Moab, they faced a different kind of enemy, one who was hidden in the mountain heights and able to call upon the forces of the evil one to assist him. Camping peacefully in the valley, the Israelites had no idea that Balaam was trying to curse them so that the Moabites and Midianites could defeat them. This scenario reminds us of Paul's warning in Ephesians 6:12, "For we wrestle not against flesh and blood, but against principalities, against powers, against the rulers of the darkness of this world [age], against spiritual wickedness in high [heavenly] places."

Satan often comes as a lion who devours (1 Peter 5:8), but if that fails, he will attack again as a serpent who deceives (2 Cor.

11:3). The church today battles against a strong enemy who has an organized army of evil spirits, dedicated to opposing God's people and God's work (Eph. 6:10-20).[1] It was this attack of the "principalities and powers" from which the Lord protected Israel as they camped on the plains of Moab.

In this study, we will consider two of the four aspects of this evil man's life and conduct and see how they relate to God and the people of Israel.

1. Balaam and God's will (Num. 22:1-35)

The key performer in this drama is a mysterious soothsayer[2] named Balaam, a Gentile who lived at a place called Pethor near the Euphrates River (v. 5; Deut. 23:4). He had a reputation for success in divination (receiving hidden knowledge, especially about the future) and incantation (the use of occult power to grant blessing or cursing), and he was willing to sell his services to all who could pay his fee.

The king's request (Num. 22:1-21). The Moabites and Midianites became very frightened when they saw the magnitude of the camp of Israel ("they cover the face of the earth," v. 5) and heard the reports of Israel's military victories over the neighboring nations ("as an ox licks up the grass of the fields," v. 4, NKJV). Balak, king of Moab, didn't realize that God had told Israel not to attack Moab (Deut. 2:9) because the Moabites were relatives of the Jews, being descendants of Abraham's nephew Lot (Gen. 19:26-37).

Conventional warfare was out of the question. Moab and Midian needed the help of the devil, and Balaam was in touch with the devil. This confrontation would be another episode in what Donald Grey Barnhouse called "the invisible war," the conflict between the Lord and Satan that began when God cursed the serpent in the garden (3:13-15; see Rev. 12). Balaam must have had a wide reputation as a successful practitioner of occult arts, otherwise Balak wouldn't have ignored both distance[3] and price when he sent for him.

Balak depended on two things to influence Balaam to come

and help him: the impressive delegation of important elders from both Midian and Moab, and the wealth they carried to pay his fee. Balaam was definitely a hireling who was interested primarily in money (2 Peter 2:15). Though twice he refused to accept Balak's summons, Balaam deceptively maneuvered around God's declared will so that he could go to Moab and receive his fee.

In those days, people believed that each nation had its own god, and Balaam knew that Jehovah was the God of the Israelites. Therefore, he went to seek the Lord's will about the summons from Balak.[4] It was God who came to Balaam, not Balaam who brought God to himself, and the Lord wouldn't allow him to accept the invitation. God made His will very clear: "Do not go with them. You must not put a curse on those people, because they are blessed" (Num. 22:12, NIV). Balaam knew that without the God of Israel on his side, he would fail in his assignment, so he told the delegation he wouldn't go with them. *However, he didn't tell them the reason: Israel couldn't be cursed because God had blessed them.* If he had told this to the delegation, that would have put an end to the negotiations and the princes would never have returned to Pethor.

Undaunted in his pursuit of victory over Israel, Balak sent Balaam a larger and even more impressive delegation of princes with the promise of paying any fee Balaam asked, plus bestowing royal honors on him. Knowing God's will in the matter, Balaam should have refused even to consider this second offer, but the hireling soothsayer was still hoping to find some way to circumvent God's will. In light of the fact that Balaam even considered the new offer, his speech in verse 18 is just so much pious talk. With his lips, he professed to obey the Lord, but in his heart he coveted the money and hoped God would change His mind.

God came to Balaam and instructed him to go with the princes *only if they came to call him the next morning* (v. 20).[5] The Lord cautioned Balaam, "Do only what I tell you." But the next morning, Balaam didn't wait for the men to come to him; he saddled his donkey and went to the place where the delegation was camped, determined to do his own will. This determination, along with the covetousness in Balaam's heart, made the Lord angry. Balaam was acting like the horse and the mule (Ps. 32:9): he was impetuously running ahead of the Lord and at the same time stubbornly refusing to obey God's clear directions. He knew that Israel was blessed, but he hoped he could curse the Jewish nation and earn the wealth and honors the king had promised him. He was a hypocrite and a double-minded man.

The donkey's resistance (Num 22:22-30). God was angry at Balaam for defying His will and allowing the love of money to control him. We sometimes use the phrase "dumb animals," but in this case the animal was smarter than her master and his two servants! She saw the angel of the Lord holding a sword and blocking the way; and by turning aside, she saved Balaam's life. Three times she changed the route and three times her master beat her. Balaam was beside himself with anger; and had he been armed, he would have killed his faithful beast. Peter called it "the madness of the prophet" (2 Peter 2:16).

Why wasn't Balaam shocked when his beast spoke to him "with a man's voice"? (v. 16, NIV) This certainly wasn't an everyday occurrence even for a professional soothsayer. Satan spoke through a serpent when he deceived Eve (Gen. 3:1ff; 2 Cor. 11:3), and it's possible that in the past Satan's demons had spoken to Balaam through animals. A person has reached a very low level in life if God has to use brute beasts to communicate His mind.

The angel's revelation (Num. 22:31-35). The same God who opened the donkey's mouth and eyes also opened Balaam's eyes so he could see the awesome angel standing in the road, his sword in hand. Balaam finally did something right and fell on his face before the angel who told him that his beast had saved his life. The angel warned Balaam that he was rushing headlong and recklessly on a wrong path that could only lead to ruin, and Balaam offered to return home.

His words, "I have sinned," were not evidence of sincere repentance. Pharaoh (Ex. 9:27), King Saul (1 Sam. 15:24, 30; 26:21), and Judas Iscariot (Matt. 27:4) all uttered these words but didn't turn to God for mercy. What good is it to say pious words if your heart goes right on sinning? Listen to David (2 Sam. 12:13; Ps. 54:4; 2 Sam. 24:10, 17; 1 Chron. 21:8, 17) or the Prodigal Son if you want to hear real confession.

In His permissive will, God allowed Balaam to continue on his journey, but He cautioned him to speak only the messages that God gave him. For the first time, Balaam realized that there was more involved in this adventure than cursing a nation and making some money. As the Lord used the donkey to rebuke her master, God would use Balaam to reveal great truths about Israel and Israel's promised Messiah.[6]

2. Balaam and God's message (Num. 22:36–24:25)

For the king to hasten out to meet the commoner shows how anxious Balak was to get started in his attack against Israel. Why had Balaam delayed his coming? Wasn't Balak's offer generous enough? Didn't the prophet realize the seriousness of the situation? Balaam didn't defend himself or explain his actions, but he did state clearly that all he could do was declare the words God gave him. The king offered sacrifices to his god Baal and probably gave Balaam some of the inner parts of the animals to use for divination.

The first oracle (Num. 22:39–23:12). The next morning, Balak took Balaam to Bamoth Baal ("the high places of Baal") where they could see the camp of Israel and offer more sacrifices to Baal. Balaam used these sacrifices as part of his sorcery and soothsaying (24:1) and didn't simply wait for God's promised message. In His grace and goodness, God used this evil man and endured his duplicity because He had a special message to declare about His people Israel.

The message God gave to Balaam emphasized several basic truths about the people of Israel. First, God had especially blessed the people of Israel and they could not be cursed (23:7-8). This was part of God's covenant with Abraham (Gen. 12:1-3) and it has been fulfilled throughout their history. God has judged every ruler and nation that has caused His people to suffer, including

Egypt, Assyria, Babylon, and Nazi Germany.

No nation has been blessed of God like Israel, not only with material blessings and divine protection, but primarily with spiritual blessings to share with the whole world. Paul lists some of them in Romans 9:1-5. Israel gave the world the knowledge of the true and living God, the written Word of God, and Jesus Christ the Savior of the world.

Balaam's second basic truth was that the Jews were chosen by God and therefore were a nation set apart from the other nations (Num. 23:9). The Lord had declared this to Israel at Mount Sinai (Ex. 19:5-6), and the laws that He gave them at Sinai made it possible for them to live like a special people. In his farewell message to Israel, Moses also emphasizes the uniqueness of Israel as the people of God (Deut. 4:20; 14:2, 21; 26:18-19; 32:8-9; 33:3, 28-29) and reminded them that God chose them because He loved them (Num. 7:6-8). See also Leviticus 20:26; 1 Kings 8:52-53; Amos 3:2; and Isaiah 43:21.

Israel's great temptation was in wanting to be like the other nations, and this is what led to their downfall and captivity. Instead of rejoicing in their uniqueness as the people of the true and living God, they imitated their neighbors in their worship and conduct, and God had to discipline them. Instead of letting God rule as their King, they asked for a king "like all the nations" (1 Sam. 8:5), and this brought the nation into all kinds of trouble.

Unfortunately, many people in the church today have the mistaken idea that being like the world is the way to reach the world. They forget that the church is the people of God, a very special people, saved by His grace. Instead of maintaining separation (2 Cor. 6:14-7:1) they promote imitation (1 John 2:15-17; Rom. 12:2), so that it's becoming more and more difficult to distinguish the people of God from the people of the world. And yet, as Campbell Morgan reminded us, "The church did the most for the world when the church was the least like the world."

Balaam's third emphasis was on the vastness of Israel's camp, even though he was seeing only a small part of it (Num.22:41).

His use of the word "dust" reminds us of God's promises to Abraham and his descendants that they would multiply and become as numerous as the dust of the earth (Gen. 13:16; 28:14). Nations come and go, but in spite of their many trials, the people of Israel have never been destroyed. Instead, they have multiplied and today are found all over the world.

Balaam was sent to curse Israel, yet he ended his oracle by declaring that he wanted to be *like* Israel! "Let me die the death of the righteous, and let my last end be like his" (Num. 23:10). But you don't die the death of the righteous unless you live the life of the righteous, and that was something Balaam wasn't prepared to do. His love of money so controlled his life that he would do anything to get wealth. Balaam died with the wicked when Israel defeated the Midianites (31:8), and his end was eternal judgment.

When Balak complained about the oracle, Balaam had only one reply: the words came from God and that's what he had to speak. Balaam could have invented a curse and fooled Balak, but the Lord wouldn't allow him to do it, for these oracles would one day be part of God's Holy Word.

The second oracle (Num. 23:13-26). To encourage Balaam to do what he was hired to do—curse Israel—Balak asked his hired prophet to get a different perspective. He took him to the top of Mount Pisgah where again they offered sacrifices to their gods (23:13-14; see Deut. 34:1-4). The fact that Balaam participated in these pagan occult rituals shows the wickedness of his heart. He spoke the Word of God and longed for a righteous death, yet he thought nothing of using enchantments and consorting with Satan (Num. 24:1). He was a double-minded man whose chief desire was to make as much money as possible by marketing his skills.

The first oracle pictured Israel as a *chosen people* because of the love of God, and the second oracle presents them as a *conquering people* because of the faithfulness of God. God doesn't lie, so all His promises and covenants are sure; He doesn't change, so His character remains the same. He isn't weak but is able to fulfill what He promises; nobody can manipulate Him or control Him.[7] God was with the people of Israel and reigned as their King.

It was God who gave Israel their victories, beginning with their exodus from Egypt. The nation was like an ox in its strength and like a lioness and a lion in its determination to catch its prey and kill it. Therefore, no sorcery could succeed against God's people because God was at work in them and through them. "Oh, what God has done!" (23:23, NKJV)

When God looked upon Israel, He didn't behold iniquity or wickedness and therefore have reason to judge them. They were "a kingdom of priests and a holy nation" (19:6), even though He had to chasten them for their unbelief and disobedience. Believers today are God's chosen people (Eph. 1:4), hidden in Christ (Col. 3:3), clothed in His righteousness (2 Cor. 5:17, 21) and seated with Him in the heavenlies (Eph. 2:4-6). Because we are "in Christ," God sees us as His own special people (1 Peter 2:5, 9-10), and He deals with us accordingly.

Once again, God turned the curse into a blessing!

The battles God's people fight today are not with flesh and blood on earth but with Satan's hosts in the heavenlies (Eph. 6:10ff), and we can't win the victory in our own strength. We must first of all see ourselves as the people of God, purchased by the blood of Christ, indwelt by the Holy Spirit, and "more than conquerors" through Christ (Rom. 8:37). Our protection is the "whole armor of God," and our chief weapons are the Word of God and prayer (Eph. 6:13-20; Acts 6:4).

As long as Israel walked with God and obeyed His will, they were an undefeated people and God did great wonders for them. "And this is the victory that has overcome the world—our faith" (1 John 5:4, NKJV).

TEN

NUMBERS 23:27–25:18

Principalities and Powers—Part II

1. Balaam and God's message (Num. 23:27–24:25)
Balak took Balaam to the top of Peor, a mountain identified with
the pagan god Baal (25:3, 5; Deut. 4:3; Ps. 106:28-29; Hosea
9:10). The usual altars were built and the animals sacrificed, but
this time Balaam didn't try to use his sorcery. Instead, he gazed
out at the camp of Israel and the Spirit of God came upon him
and gave him the third oracle.

The third oracle (Num. 23:27–24:14). The emphasis here is on
the contentment of God's people in their own land. The conquest of Canaan is over (24:8-9), their enemies have been defeated, and Israel is enjoying the abundance of God's provision in
"the land of milk and honey." The Promised Land is a paradise
with an abundance of water, an important commodity in the
East, and Israel's dwelling places are situated like beautiful flow-
ers and trees in a garden. Beauty and bounty are seen in the land
because of the blessing of the Lord.

In the second oracle, Balaam saw God as Israel's King (23:21),
but now he sees the nation ruled by its own king who is greater
than Agag (24:7). Since the name Agag shows up centuries later
(1 Sam. 15:9), it may have been the official name of the rulers of

the Amalekites, such as "Pharaoh" in Egypt and "Abimelech" in Gerar (Gen. 20; 26). When Israel was on the way to Sinai, the Amalekites attacked them and were defeated by Moses' prayers and Joshua's soldiers, and the Amalekites became the sworn enemies of the Jews (Ex. 17:8-16).

Which Jewish king is referred to in this prophecy? Certainly not King Saul, who failed to exterminate the Amalekites and died in disgrace. Possibly, it may be David, but certainly it points to Jesus Christ who is "higher than the kings of the earth" (Ps. 89:27). There seems to be a dual prophecy here, for during the reign of Jesus Christ over the promised messianic kingdom, the land of Israel will become like the Garden of Eden (Isa. 35).

Balaam repeats the images of the ox and the lion (Num. 24:8-9; see 23:22, 24), and closes his oracle with a quotation from God's covenant with Abraham (24:9; Gen. 12:3; 27:29). Balak didn't like what he said, especially the threat of being cursed if he cursed Israel. He told the soothsayer to go home, and because Balaam didn't do the job right, he wouldn't be paid. Because Balaam listened to the Lord and spoke only His Word, King Balak concluded that the Lord had robbed Balaam of his reward!

Balaam agreed to return home, but not until he had delivered his fourth oracle. However, Balaam remained with Balak long enough to engineer the seductive feast that led to the defilement and defeat of Israel. He couldn't curse Israel but he could tempt them into compromise.

The fourth oracle (Num. 24:15-19). The preface is similar to that of the third oracle (vv. 3-4), emphasizing that what Balaam saw and heard came from the Lord. It was so overwhelming that it left the prophet prostrate on the ground. You would think that such a remarkable experience with the living God would have brought Balaam to the place of submission and faith, but it did not. It only shows how close an unbeliever can come to the knowledge of the Lord and still reject the truth (Matt. 7:15-23).[1]

The vision is brief and to the point; it focuses on the coming Messiah of Israel and His conquests "in the latter days" (Num. 24:14). The images of the star and scepter speak of Messiah's kingship and reign (Gen. 49:10; Rev. 22:16), and "out of Jacob shall He come who shall have dominion" certainly refers to Messiah (Num. 24:19; Ps. 72:8; Zech. 9:10; Rev. 1:6). While a part of this vision may have been fulfilled in a lesser way in the conquests of David, Jesus the Son of David will fulfill them completely when He returns to conquer His enemies and establish His kingdom on the earth (Rev. 19:11–20:6).

But the soothsayer wasn't finished. As he stood on the top of Peor, he had visions concerning other nations and predicted their destiny. *Amalek (Num. 24:20)* was the first nation to attack Israel after their exodus from Egypt (Ex. 17:8-16), but they would be finally defeated and wiped out by David (1 Sam. 27:8-9; 2 Sam. 8:11-12). *The Kenites (Num. 24:21-22)* were a nomadic people who lived among the Midianites.[2] They lived in the mountainous regions, but their "nest" wouldn't protect them from the invading Assyrians (Asshur) who would take them captive. The fate of the nations is in God's hands (Acts 17:24-28), and no nation or individual could survive apart from His mercy (Num. 24:23).

The predictions in verse 25 are difficult to interpret, but as Dr. Roland B. Allen states, "[O]ne nation will rise and supplant another, only to face its own doom. In contrast there is the implied ongoing blessing on the people of Israel and their sure promise of a future deliverer who will have the final victory...."[3] It is a remarkable thing that God gave this vision to a covetous Gentile soothsayer instead of to a dedicated Jewish prophet. But He is sovereign in all His ways, and His ways are higher than our ways (Isa. 55:8-11).

2. Balaam and God's people (Num. 25:1-18)

"Then Balaam got up and returned home" (24:25, NIV) shouldn't be interpreted to mean that he returned immediately to Pethor, because Balaam was among those killed when Israel slaughtered the Midianites (31:8). "Home" probably means the place where Balaam was staying while visiting Balak.

The sin of Israel (Num. 25:1-5). Balaam wasn't able to curse Israel, but he knew how to defile them and seduce them into sin so great that Jehovah would judge them. Balaam suggested to Balak (31:16) that the Moabites (25:1) and Midianites (v. 6) convene a religious feast to honor Baal, and that they invite the Jews to attend. The feast, of course, would involve idolatry and abominable immorality and would be a flagrant violation of Israel's covenant with the Lord. But Moab was related to Israel through Abraham's nephew Lot, and the Midianites were the allies of Moab, so there was no reason why the Jews shouldn't be "neighborly." What Balaam couldn't do by appealing to the demons, he accomplished by appealing to the flesh and inviting the Jews to "enjoy themselves" at Baal Peor.

This is the first recorded occasion in Scripture of Israel worshiping Baal, but it certainly isn't the last. Baal was the chief of the Canaanite gods and was especially responsible for rain and fertility. Until they went off to Babylon, the Israelites were an agricultural people; and whenever there was a drought, they often turned to Baal for help instead of to the Lord. The Canaanite fertility rites involved both male and female temple prostitutes and encouraged all kinds of sexual immorality. Both the idolatry and the immorality were forbidden by God's law (Ex. 20:1-5, 14).

You would expect the Jews to remember the nation's awesome experience at Sinai when they entered into their covenant relationship with the Lord. They would also be expected to recall the nation's idolatry at Sinai when Aaron made the golden calf and God judged the nation (Ex. 32). That event also involved both idolatry and immorality. Israel was a special people, God's "nation of priests," and they had no business mixing with the pagan Moabites and Midianites and worshiping their false gods.

The Lord sent a plague that began to kill the people, so Moses moved into action. Following God's orders, he commanded the judges in each tribe to kill the people who had led Israel into this terrible sin, and to expose their bodies as a warning to the rest of the people. But one special act of judgment helped to bring the plague to an end and save the rest of the nation.

The courage of Phinehas (Num. 25:6-15). Zimri, a leader in the tribe of Simeon (v. 14), not only attended the idolatrous feast but brought a Midianite woman named Cozbi (v. 15) back to the camp of Israel and openly took her into his tent right before the eyes of Moses and the weeping Israelites at the tabernacle door.[4] This was a brazen high-handed sin for which there was no forgiveness. Zimri was a prince in Israel and Cozbi was the daughter of a prince, so perhaps they thought their social status gave them the privilege of sinning.

Aaron's grandson Phinehas left the prayer meeting and went after the couple, killing both of them in the tent with one thrust of his spear. This stopped the plague, but not before 24,000 people had died (Deut. 4:3-4).[5] Like Abraham when he offered up Isaac (Gen. 22; James 2:21-24), Phinehas proved his faith by his works, and it was "accounted to him for righteousness" (Ps. 106:28-31).

Because of his zeal for the honor of the Lord, Phinehas was given the special reward of a lasting priesthood for himself and his descendants. Phinehas knew nothing about this reward before he acted, so his motive wasn't selfish. He was motivated by his zeal for the honor of God and the authority of His Law. Phinehas went with Moses when Israel attacked the Midianites (Num. 31:5-6), so he wasn't afraid of a battle. He also was in charge of the gatekeepers at the tabernacle and had the presence of the Lord with him in his ministry (1 Chron. 9:20). Guarding God's sanctuary was a very responsible task, but Phinehas had the conviction and courage to do it well.

The judgment of Midian (Num. 25:16-18). God declared that the Midianites were to be considered the enemies of Israel and had to be killed. The account of Moses' fulfilling this order is in 31:1-24. As we've already noted, Balaam, the man who masterminded the feast, was killed at the same time.

Those who criticize the Lord and Scripture because of these national massacres fail to understand that God had been patient with these wicked nations for centuries (Gen. 15:16) and had given them ample opportunity to repent. He had revealed

Himself to them in nature (Rom. 1:18ff; Ps. 19), and they had heard of the Lord's judgments against Egypt (Josh. 2:8-14). Their religious practices were abominably filthy, and the only way God could remove this cancer was to wipe out the entire civilization. Israel had an important task to perform for the Lord, and the presence of those wicked nations was only a temptation to the Jews to sin.

3. Balaam and today's church

As God's people today, we must not think that the Old Testament narratives are past history and simply interesting stories for us to read. Until the New Testament was written, the only Scriptures the first-century church had was the Old Testament; and from it they were able to get encouragement and enlightenment. These events in Jewish history serve as warnings to us not to disobey the Lord (1 Cor. 10:1-13) as well as encouragements to build our faith (Heb. 11) and hope (Rom. 15:4).

Balaam is mentioned by three different New Testament writers: Peter (2 Peter 2:15-16), Jude (v. 11), and John (Rev. 2:14).

"The way of Balaam" (2 Peter 2:15-16). The second chapter of 2 Peter focuses on the danger of false teachers secretly entering the church and leading people astray. Peter promises that God will judge these deceivers (v. 3), but he also warns the believers to exercise spiritual discernment lest they be taken captive by false doctrine. These false teachers are like Balaam in that they knew the right way but turned from it, they were covetous, and they led people into immorality (v. 14). In fact, as you read the chapter, you will see the characteristics of Balaam exposed.

The "way of Balaam" is Balaam's lifestyle as a soothsayer and false prophet. His motive was to make money and he used his opportunities, not to serve God and His people, but to satisfy his craving for wealth. In other words, he was a hireling who sold himself to the highest bidder. He used "religion" only to make money and to cover up his sinful cravings. He also used "religion" to entice people to sin.

Balaam knew that God didn't want him to go with the delegation and serve King Balak, but he maneuvered around God's declared will and went to Moab. The British minister F.W. Robertson said, "He went to God to get his duty altered, not to learn was his duty was."[6] No matter what he said with his lips, Balaam had a hidden agenda that really wasn't hidden from God at all. If God isn't allowed to rule in a person's life, He overrules and accomplishes His purposes just the same, *but the disobedient servant is the loser.*

God used the "dumb animal" to rebuke Balaam and try to get him on the right track, but Balaam's heart never changed. The sight of the angel of the Lord may have frightened him, but it didn't bring him to surrender and faith. Balak had promised him great wealth and he was going to get it one way or another.

When are we walking on "the way of Balaam"? When we deliberately rebel against the revealed will of God and try to change it. When we have selfish motives and ask, "What will I get out of it?" When we cause other people to sin so we can profit from it. Paul may have had Balaam in mind when he wrote 1 Timothy 6:9-10, words that need to be taken seriously today. "Religion" is "big business" today and it's easy for preachers, musicians, executives, writers, and others in Christian service to become more concerned with money and reputation than spiritual values and Christian character.

"The error of Balaam" (Jude 11). Like Peter, Jude wrote to warn the church about false teachers (vv. 3-4). In fact, Jude's letter is an echo of what Peter wrote in 2 Peter 2, so the Lord has given us a double warning. This shows us how serious the danger is and how great is our responsibility to detect and defeat these insidious false teachers. Unfortunately, many professed believers care little about Bible doctrine and easily fall prey to heretical influences. It's a known fact that many members of false cults were once members of orthodox churches. Cultists don't try to win lost souls, because they have no salvation message for the lost. Instead, they capture new converts and bring them into bondage (vv. 18-19).

Balaam's error was not only thinking that he could disobey

God and get away with it, but also in thinking that those he enticed to sin would get away with it. The false teachers in the days of Peter and Jude preyed upon ignorant people and tried to lead them into sin (vv. 10, 13, 18; Jude 4, 8, 18-19), all the time covering everything over with a cloak of "religion." If the greatest evil is the corruption of the highest good, then these false teachers were indeed the greatest of sinners, for they used the Christian faith as a cloak for their wicked deeds.

Of course, "reward" was the motivation behind what they did (v. 11), and this could mean a number of things: money, power over people, popularity, and personal sensual pleasure. Judas Iscariot used ministry for personal gain (John 12:6) but ended up a suicide.

"The doctrine of Balaam" (Rev. 2:14). This is the doctrine Balaam followed when he enticed Israel to attend the idolatrous feast at Baal Peor and commit immorality with the Midianites (Num. 25). The world would express it, "When in Rome, do as the Romans do. Don't be a 'holier than thou' isolationist. Be a good neighbor and a good sport. After all, you live in a pluralistic society, so learn to respect the way other people believe and live." But from God's point of view, what Israel did was *compromise* and a violation of their covenant made at Sinai.

The problem at Pergamos was that the false teachers had gotten into the church and were enticing people to attend the feasts at the idol temples.[7] As at Baal Peor, their sin was a combination of idolatry and immorality, but the false teachers didn't present it that way. They taught that God's grace gave His people the freedom to sin, but Jude called it "turning the grace of God into lasciviousness" (Jude 4; and see Rom. 6:1ff).

The Jews were God's chosen people, set apart from the rest of the nations to serve and glorify Him. They were not to worship the gods of their neighbors or share in their pagan festivities. When they entered the Promised Land, they were to tear down the pagan temples and altars and destroy the idols (Deut. 7; Josh. 23), lest Israel be tempted to turn from the true and living God and start imitating the heathen neighbors. Unfortunately, that's exactly what happened after the death of Joshua (Jud. 2:10-3:6).

The doctrine of Balaam is the lie that it's permissible for saved people to live like unsaved people, that God's grace gives us the right to disobey God's Law. Throughout the Old Testament, Israel's compromise with idolatry is called "adultery" and "playing the harlot," for the nation was "married" to Jehovah at Sinai. (See Jer. 2:19-20; 3:1-11; Ezek. 16; 23; and Hosea 1–2.) This same "marriage" image is applied to Christ and the church in the New Testament (2 Cor. 11:1-4; Eph. 5:22-33; James 4:4; Rev. 19:6-9). The believer compromising with sin is like the husband or wife committing adultery.

Any teaching that makes it easy and permissible to sin is false doctrine, because the Word of God was given to us to enable us to live holy lives (1 Tim. 6:3-4; Titus 1:1). Paul emphasized the need in the church for "sound doctrine," which means "healthy doctrine" (1 Tim. 1:10; 2 Tim. 4:3; Titus 1:9; 2:1).[8] False doctrine he compared to a cancerous growth (2 Tim. 2:17, NKJV).

When Israel killed Balaam centuries ago, they couldn't kill the lies he turned loose in the world, lies that still influenced the Jews after they had conquered Canaan (Josh. 22:15-18). These lies influence individual believers and churches today and the cancer of compromise weakens our witness and saps our spiritual strength (2 Cor. 6:14-7:1).

We must heed the warning of F.W. Robertson: "Brethren, beware. See how a man may be going on uttering fine words, orthodox truths, and yet be rotten at the heart."[9]

"Keep your heart with all diligence, for out of it spring the issues of life" (Prov. 4:23, NKJV).

ELEVEN

A New Beginning

The transition between chapters 25 and 26 reminds us of the transition from chapter 14 to chapter 15, for in both of them the Lord moved from judgment to mercy, from punishment to promise. At Kadesh-Barnea and at Baal Peor, Israel had sinned greatly and God chastened them, but in His grace He forgave their disobedience and gave them a new start. Ezra the scribe expressed this truth in his prayer of confession when he said, "You our God have punished us less than our iniquities deserve" (Ezra 9:13, NKJV); David felt the same way when he wrote, "He does not treat us as our sins deserve or repay us according to our iniquities" (Ps. 103:10, NIV).

As Israel lingered in the plains of Moab, Moses fulfilled four important responsibilities to prepare Israel for what lay ahead.

1. Numbering the soldiers (Num. 26:1-51)

By the time Israel had entered the Zared valley (21:12), the old generation had died off (Deut. 2:14-15), except for Moses, Caleb, and Joshua (Num. 26:63-65); and very soon, Moses would die. Israel was making a new beginning, thanks to the faithfulness and mercy of God. It was time to take a census of the new generation and start looking toward the future.

Moses had two purposes in mind when he took the second census.[1] As with the first census (1:1-46), Moses needed to know how many men were available, twenty years and older, who could serve in the army. The second purpose for the census was to get an idea of how much land each tribe would need when Israel settled down in Canaan and claimed their inheritance (26:52-56). Assigning each tribe its inheritance would be the task of Joshua, Eleazar the high priest, and ten leaders representing the tribes that were settling west of the Jordan River (34:16-29).

The first census had revealed a total of 603,550 available soldiers (1:45-46), while the second census totaled 601,730 (26:51), a slight decrease. When you consider that every man had now been replaced who had died during the previous thirty-eight years *except for only 1,820 men*, this total is quite remarkable. Just as God had multiplied His people during their years of suffering in Egypt (Ex. 1:7, 12), so He made them fruitful during their years of traveling in the wilderness. The Lord was faithful to keep His covenant promise (Gen. 12:2; 15:5; 22:17).

The available soldiers dropped in number in the tribes of Gad, Simeon, and Reuben, with the tribe of Simeon showing the biggest drop, from 59,300 to 22,2000. These three tribes camped together on the south side of the tabernacle and may have been a bad influence on each other. Dathan and Abiram belonged to the tribe of Reuben and were part of Korah's rebellion during which nearly 15,000 people died (Num. 26:9-11; 16:35, 49). Perhaps many of the rebels came from that tribe. Also, Zimri, who arrogantly sinned in the matter of Baal Peor (25:6-15), was a prince in the tribe of Simeon. His evil example may have influenced other men of Simeon to share in the Midianite idolatry and immorality, for which sins they too perished.

Judah, Issachar, and Zebulun, who encamped on the east side of the tabernacle, all showed significant gains. It's strange that Ephraim lost 8,000 people while the brother tribe of Manasseh gained 20,000.

God could have sent angels to clean up Canaan instantly, but

He chose to work through human beings, a day at a time. God is certainly long-suffering toward His people, and we ought to count it a great privilege to know Him and be able to work with Him in doing His work.

2. Preparing for the inheritance (Num. 26:52–27:11; 36)

Israel had not yet crossed the river and entered the Promised Land, and yet by faith Moses was already preparing for the tribes to claim their land. (The words "inherit" or "inheritance" are used twelve times in this section.) Except for fulfilling God's command to wipe out the Midianites (25:16-18; 31:1-11), Israel would have no more battles until they arrived at Jericho. Though he wasn't allowed to go in himself, Moses invested the closing weeks of his life in preparing the new generation to enter Canaan and claim the land God promised to give them.

The tribal inheritance (Num. 26:52-56). Once the land had been conquered and God had given His people rest, Joshua, Eleazar, and the ten tribal representatives (34:16-29) would cast lots to determine each tribe's portion of the land (Josh. 14–19). Naturally, the size of the tribe would help to establish the amount of land that would be assigned. According to the record in the Book of Joshua, some of the tribes gladly accepted their inheritance and went to work making it "home," some complained about the land they were given, and some went out and conquered more territory. "According to your faith be it unto you" (Matt. 9:29).[2]

The levitical inheritance (Num. 26:57-62). From the first census to the second, the number of Levites increased slightly from 22,000 (3:39) to 23,000 (27:62). The Levites were not given their own territory to possess but were scattered throughout the nation in forty-eight assigned cities (35:1-5; Josh. 21). There were at least three reasons for this procedure.

First, scattering the Levites fulfilled Jacob's deathbed prophecy that Levi's descendants would be distributed throughout the land (Gen. 49:1-7). Levi and Simeon had been violent in their treatment of the people of Shechem (Gen. 34), and Jacob felt it would be safer if the sons of Levi were widely dispersed.

Second, by scattering throughout the land, the Levites had a better opportunity to teach the Law to more people and influence them to be faithful to the Lord. Parents were obligated to teach their children God's Word (Deut. 4:1-10; 6:6-15), but it was the responsibility of the priests and Levites to teach the people the meaning of God's Law and the blessing of obeying it (Lev. 10:11; 2 Chron. 15:3; 17:7; Mal. 2:4-7).

The third reason the Levites were not allowed to inherit property was that God was their inheritance (Num. 26:62). They were privileged to serve God by assisting the priests, and they shared in the sacrifices and tithes that the people brought to the Lord (18:20; Deut. 10:9; 12:12; 14:27-29; 18:1-2; Josh. 13:14, 33). The Levites were to devote themselves wholly to the service of the Lord and His people and to live by faith, receiving what they needed from God's hand through His people.

The family inheritance (Num. 27:1-11). Since the land belonged to the Lord (Lev. 25:23-28), the Jews couldn't divide it or dispose of it as they pleased. Maintaining the inheritance from generation to generation was important to each family and to the tribes to which the families belonged.[3]

As with the other nations of that day, Israel was a strongly masculine society, and fathers left their property to their sons. The eldest son received two-thirds of the inheritance and the other sons divided the remaining one-third (Deut. 21:15-17). If a man didn't have a son, he left his estate to his nearest male relative, but not to a daughter. When a daughter was married, she received a dowry from her father and would no longer live in the family home. The dowry was her inheritance.

The five daughters of Zelophehad, of the tribe of Manasseh, thought that this law of inheritance was unfair, and they asked Moses, Eleazar, the tribal princes, and the whole congregation to consider changing it. Why should their father's name be blotted out of Israel because of something over which he had no control? Should his family be penalized because he had no son?

Being a wise man, Moses took the matter to the Lord, just as he had done with the problem of the blasphemer (Lev. 24:10-16) and the man who violated the Sabbath (Num. 15:32-36). The Lord agreed with the five women and decreed that a father who had no son could leave his estate to his daughter. If he had neither son nor daughter, he could pass the land on to his nearest male relative.

The decision to allow daughters to inherit solved one problem but created another one, and the leaders of the tribe of Manasseh called it to the attention of Moses (Num. 36). If a daughter who had inherited her father's land married into another tribe, this would take the land away from the original tribe and make it part of her husband's estate. At the Year of Jubilee (Lev. 25:8-24), it could not return to the original family, and this would rob a tribe of its property.

Moses must have taken the matter to the Lord, because he replied "according to the word of the Lord" (Num. 27:5). The solution was to require daughters who had the inheritance to marry men who belonged to their own tribe. This simple procedure would permit the daughters to marry but would at the same time keep family property in the original tribe. The five sisters obeyed the edict and each one married a cousin.

Regulations like this are unnecessary in today's society, but they were very important to God's ancient people. God owned the land and allowed His people to use it as long as they obeyed Him. When the Jews turned to idols and polluted the land, God allowed other nations to invade and steal the produce (see the Book of Judges). When Israel's sins became so heinous that God could endure it no longer, He took the Jews off the land and exiled them to Babylon. There they learned to appreciate what the Lord had given to them.

To the Jews in Canaan, possessing land was the foundation for building a family, earning an income, and having security and the necessities of life. The prophets frequently denounced wealthy people who amassed great estates by stealing land from the poor (Isa. 5:8-10; Micah 2:1-3; Hab. 2:9-12). The ideal life for an Old Testament Jew was to own his own land and be able to sit under his own fig tree and enjoy his family and the fruit of his labor (1 Kings 4:25; Micah 4:4).

3. Dedicating a new leader (Num. 27:12-23)

Though still physically strong, Moses was now 120 years old (Deut. 31:2; 34:7) and the time had come for him to move off the scene. He had led the people of Israel faithfully for forty years (Acts 7:23, 30; Ex. 7:7), bearing their burdens, sharing their victories, and teaching them God's laws. God and Moses communed with each other as friend with friend, and the Lord didn't hide anything from His servant.

Moses and the land (Num. 27:12-14). Because Moses and Aaron had not honored the Lord at Meribah, they weren't permitted to enter the Promised Land with the new generation (20:2-13). Moses repeatedly asked God for permission to enter the land (Deut. 4:23-29),[4] but the Lord refused to relent. Not only must Moses be disciplined because of his pride and anger at Meribah, but he must not mar the type that would be expounded in the Book of Hebrews. It isn't the Law (Moses) that gives us our spiritual inheritance but Jesus (Joshua; Heb. 4:8; and context).[5]

After Moses delivered the messages recorded in Deuteronomy, he was permitted to ascend Mount Nebo (Pisgah), in the Abarim mountain range, and view the land that Israel would inherit (Deut. 32:48-52; 34:1-4). Centuries later, Moses and Elijah would stand in glory on the Mount of Transfiguration when they talked with Jesus about His impending death on the cross (Matt. 17:1-8); so he did finally make it to the Promised Land.

Moses and Joshua (Num. 27:15-23). Many times during his long ministry, Moses had proved himself a true leader by being more concerned for the people than for himself. Twice God had offered to destroy the Jews and start a new nation with Moses, but Moses had refused (14:11-19; Ex. 32:7-14), and often he had interceded for the people when God's judgment was about to fall. He had been misunderstood, criticized, and nearly stoned, but he remained a faithful shepherd to his people.

Though he was about to die, Moses didn't think about himself but about the future of the nation. His great concern was that God provide a spiritual leader for the people, for they were sheep (Num. 27:17; see Pss. 74:1; 79:13; 95:7; 100:3; 2 Sam. 24:7), and sheep must have a shepherd (1 Kings 22:17; Zech. 10:2; Matt. 9:36; Mark 6:34).

It was certainly no surprise that Joshua was the man God chose to take Moses' place, for Joshua had worked closely with Moses since the nation left Egypt. He led the Jewish army in defeating the Amalekites (Ex. 17:8-16), and he ministered as Moses' servant (24:13; 33:11; Num. 11:28), even going up Sinai with Moses when God gave the Law (v. 13; 32:17). As one of the twelve spies, he joined with Caleb in encouraging the people to enter the land (Num. 14:6-9). He was filled with the Spirit (27:18; Deut. 34:9) and had been disciplined in the rigors of Egyptian slavery and the wilderness march. In every way, he was a perfect successor to Moses.

Moses had received his call and commission in the loneliness of the Midianite wilderness (Ex. 3), but Joshua was commissioned publicly by Moses and Eleazar the high priest. Moses laid his hand on his successor and bestowed on him the authority God had given him, and Eleazar would use the Urim and Thummin to help Joshua determine the will of God (28:30). In the weeks that followed, Moses gradually gave more responsibility to Joshua so that the people learned to respect him and obey him as God's chosen leader.[6] Part of Moses' commissioning speech is found in Deuteronomy 31:1-8, and God gave Joshua further encouragement in Joshua 1:1-9.

During his years of service with Moses, Joshua learned some valuable principles of spiritual life and service, principles that still apply today. When you read the Book of Joshua, you see that he was concerned for the glory of God and the welfare of the people, and that he was careful to obey the orders God gave him. The two times Joshua didn't seek God's will, he brought the nation into shameful defeat (Josh. 7 and 9), but to his credit, he trusted God to make his mistakes work out successfully in the end.

Under Joshua's leadership, the nation worked together to defeat the pagan nations in Canaan and then establish the nation of Israel. Before he died, he called the leaders and the people together and led them in dedicating themselves and their families to the Lord, affirming to them, "As for me and my house, we will serve the Lord" (24:15).

One of the responsibilities of Christian leaders today is to see to it that the next generation is equipped to carry on the work (2 Tim. 2:2). Each local church is just one generation short of extinction, and unless we teach and train new leaders, we jeopardize the future of our homes, churches, and nation.

4. Focusing on worship (Num. 28:1–29:40)

From the beginning of their national life, the secret of Israel's success was a relationship to the Lord characterized by faith and obedience. The Jews were God's covenant people, chosen by Him to do His will and ultimately bring the Redeemer into the world. Once Israel was settled in the land, they had to be careful to follow these instructions carefully, for they worshiped the Lord God Almighty. The pagan nations around them could invent their own forms of worship, but Israel had to bring the right sacrifices at the right time and in the right way, or the Lord could not bless them (John 4:22).

Some of the instructions given here had already been given at Sinai, while others were new. The basis for their worship was the calendar of special days outlined in Leviticus 23, beginning with the weekly Sabbath and ending with the annual Feast of Tabernacles.[7] The phrase "sweet savour" in the KJV, used seven times in these two chapters (Num. 28:2, 6, 8, 13; 29:2, 6, 8), is translated "an aroma pleasing to Me" in the NIV. Each of the offerings had a different purpose to fulfill, but the ultimate goal was to please the Lord and delight His heart. God seeks for true worshipers (John 4:23) and delights in the worship of His loving people.

Daily sacrifices (Num. 28:1-10). Each morning and each evening, the priests were to offer a lamb as a burnt offering. The new instruction was that on the Sabbath days they were to offer two lambs each morning and evening. (See Ex. 29:38-43 and Lev. 1.) The burnt offering typified total dedication to the Lord, and we should begin and end each day by giving ourselves completely to the Lord (Rom. 12:1-2). The Christian life is a "continual burnt offering," except that we are *living* sacrifices not dead ones.

Monthly offerings (Num. 28:11-15). This was a new instruction to the priests. The Jewish people followed a lunar calendar (Lev. 23) and "new moon" was joyfully celebrated by the nation as a whole (Num. 10:10; Ps. 81:1-3) as well as by individual families (1 Sam. 20:5, 18, 24). On the first of every month, along with the daily continual burnt offering, the priests were to offer an additional burnt offering comprised of two young bulls, a ram, and seven male lambs a year old, along with the proper meal offerings and drink offerings. A male goat was also sacrificed as a sin offering. Israel was to make a new start with each new month.

Offerings for the annual religious events (Num. 28:16–29:40). Five different annual events are named here, starting with Passover. Pentecost was celebrated seven weeks after Passover (pentecost means "fiftieth day" in Greek), and was also called "The Feast of Weeks." The seventh month of the Jewish year opened with the Feast of Trumpets (29:1-6; Lev. 23:23-25), signaling the beginning of the Jewish civil year (Rosh Hashana). On the tenth day of that month, Israel celebrated the Day of Atonement (Num. 29:7-11; Lev. 16; 23:26-32). Five days later, the Feast of Tabernacles began and lasted for a week. It was a joyful time of harvest celebration when the Jews lived in booths to commemorate their time in the wilderness. For each of these special events, the priests were instructed to offer appropriate sacrifices. For believers today, these special annual events speak of Christ and what He has done for us.

Passover (Num. 28:16-25; Ex. 12). This feast celebrated Israel's exodus from Egypt and also marked the beginning of the nation's religious year (Ex. 12, and note v. 2). On the fourteenth day of the month, the head of each household brought a lamb to be slain and later roasted and eaten, but on the fifteenth day, the priests had to offer on the altar sacrifices identical to those offered at new moon: a burnt offering of two young bulls, one ram, and seven male lambs, plus a male goat for a sin offering. Identical sacrifices were repeated each day for a week, during which time the Jews celebrated the Feast of Unleavened Bread and removed all traces of yeast from their homes.

For the Christian believer, Passover speaks of the death of Christ on the cross for the sins of the world (John 1:29; 1 Cor. 5:7-8; 1 Peter 1:18-21; Rev. 5:5-6). Yeast is a picture of sin, and God's redeemed people must put sin out of their lives and be a holy people (1 Cor. 5:1-8; Gal. 5:7-9; Matt. 16:6; Mark 8:15; Luke 12:1).

Pentecost (Num. 28:26-30; Lev. 23:15-22) was celebrated fifty days after Passover, counting from the Feast of Firstfruits, which was the day after the Sabbath following Passover.[8] The priest offered sacrifices identical to those offered for new moon and Passover. Christians celebrate Pentecost as the day when the promised Holy Spirit came and baptized believers into the body of Christ and filled them with power for ministry (Acts 1:1-5; 2:1-4). Pentecost is the birthday of the church.

The Feast of Trumpets (Num. 29:1-6; Lev. 23:23-25). The blowing of the trumpets on the first day of the seventh month signaled the beginning of a new civil year for Israel. On that day the Jews were not to work and the priests were to offer a burnt offering of one bull, one ram, and seven male lambs, as well as a sin offering of one male goat.

According to Numbers 10, the trumpets could be blown for several reasons: to call the people together (v. 2), to sound an alarm (v. 5), or to announce a battle (v. 9). Today, the Jews are a scattered people (Deut. 28; Lev. 26), but one day the trumpet will sound to call them back to their land and prepare them for the return of their Messiah (Isa. 27:12-13; Matt. 24:29, 31). The trumpet sound that Christians are awaiting will announce the return of the Savior for His church (1 Thes. 4:13-18).

The Day of Atonement (Num. 29:7-11; Lev. 16; 23:26-32).

This was Israel's highest and holiest day, when the people fasted and abstained from all work. The priest offered sacrifices identical to those offered on the first day of the month, but he also *by himself* followed the ceremony outlined in Leviticus 16. This was the only day of the year when the high priest was permitted to go beyond the veil into the holy of holies, but he had to bring with him burning incense and sacrificial blood. The ritual on the Day of Atonement pictures the work of Jesus Christ when He died on the cross for our sins.

The Feast of Tabernacles (Num. 29:12-39; Lev. 23:33-43). This joyful harvest festival began five days after the Day of Atonement and lasted for a week. During that week, the priests offered over 200 sacrifices, including the daily burnt offerings (2 lambs) which were doubled on the Sabbath. This feast looks forward to the time when God will fulfill the kingdom promises made to Israel and the nation will rejoice in their bountiful beautiful land.

Believers today can learn at least three practical lessons from these offerings. First, all of them are fulfilled in Jesus Christ (Heb. 10:1-18). The blood of animals can never take away sin (vv. 1-4), but the blood of Christ cleanses us from all sin (1 John 1:7; Eph. 1:7; Rev. 1:5). These sacrifices had to be repeated on a regular schedule; but the sacrifice of Jesus Christ at Calvary accomplished eternal salvation once for all (Heb. 9:24-28; 10:11-14).

Second, the nation could not have functioned without the ministry of the priests. They represented the people before God and offered the sacrifices that He required. Today, Jesus Christ is the believer's high priest in heaven (4:14-16) and "ever lives to make intercession for us" (7:25). His sacrifice at Calvary was final, and now He is our high priest, advocate (1 John 2:1-3), and mediator in heaven (1 Tim. 2:5; Heb. 8:6; 12:24).

Third, these sacrifices were very expensive. Totally apart from the sacrifices that the people brought in their own personal worship, and the great number of lambs slain at Passover, each year the priests offered 113 bulls, 32 rams, and 1,086 lambs! If God's people under Law could do this, how much more should we do who have experienced the grace of God!

How thankful we should be that the ancient sacrificial system has been fulfilled in Jesus Christ, and that we have the privilege of coming into the presence of God at any time through the new and living way (10:19-25). As priests of God, we can bring to Him our spiritual sacrifices (1 Peter 2:5, 9): our bodies (Rom. 12:1-2), people won to Christ (15:16), money and material gifts (Phil. 4:18), worship and praise (Heb. 13:15), good works (v. 16), a broken heart (Ps. 51:17), and believing prayer (141:1-2).

Let's imitate David and not give to the Lord that which costs us nothing (2 Sam. 24:24; see Mal. 1:6-11).

TWELVE

Preparing for Conquest

For forty years, Israel had been moving from place to place, a nomadic people traveling to their Promised Land. Soon they would enter and conquer that land and establish their own nation, and for this responsibility they had to be prepared. The final chapters of Numbers, along with the Book of Deuteronomy, record the Lord's instructions through Moses, given to prepare the people for this challenging new experience. For Israel to become a holy nation to the glory of God, they had to accept and apply the basic principles Moses enunciated, and these principles still work in communities and nations today.

1. The sanctity of words (Num. 30:1-16)

In Leviticus 27 Moses had touched on the subject of vows in terms of dedicating people and possessions to the Lord, but here he deals with personal vows and how they are affected by relationships. The chapter makes it clear that the home is basic to the nation, that there must be authority and subordination in the home, and that truth is what binds society together.

There is a difference between "vows" and "oaths," but both were to be considered inviolate. The vow was a promise to do a certain thing for the Lord, while the oath was a promise not to do a certain thing. Any man who made a vow or took an oath had to keep his word, because what he said was "unto the Lord." When people forget that God hears what they say, then they're tempted to deceive, and lies cause the fabric of society to rip apart. (See Deut. 23:21; Ps. 76:11; Ecc. 5:1-7.)

When the men made promises to God, they had to keep their promises and nobody could annul them, but what about the women? Moses deals with the vows of single women at home (Num. 30:3-8), women formerly married (v. 9), and married women (vv. 10-15). The basic principle is that if the woman was under the authority of her father or husband, the father or husband had to approve the vow. He also had the power to cancel the vow.

The single young woman at home (Num. 30:3-8). If the father hears the vow and says nothing, the vow must stand and the young lady must fulfill it. Not only is there power in words, but there's also power in silence; in this case, silence means consent. But if the father announces that he disapproves of the vow, then the vow is canceled. If later she becomes engaged to be married and her fiancé knows about the vow and says nothing, then the vow stands, even after they marry, but if he doesn't approve, the vow is annulled even if her father approved it. The Lord would then release her from the obligations related to that vow.

The widow and the divorcee (Num. 30:9). The Lord assumes that these women are experienced and mature and can make wise decisions, although age and experience aren't always a guarantee of wisdom. If they make promises to the Lord, these promises must be fulfilled. Moses doesn't explain what would happen if they married again. Since no special qualifications are given, we assume that their vows couldn't be canceled even by their new husbands.

The married woman (Num. 30:10-16). If the husband hears the vow and says nothing, the vow becomes binding, for silence means consent. If he openly disagrees with the vow and forbids it, the vow is annulled. However, if he should change his mind after consenting, then he (not the wife) must pay the penalty for causing her to abandon her sacred vow, and this meant bringing a sin offering to the Lord (Lev. 5:4).

Written into this ruling are some important truths, not the least of which is the power of speech. To make a promise is to obligate oneself to the Lord, whether people realize this or not. The foundations of society today are eroding because of unkept promises, whether they be official contracts, marriage vows, political pledges, or words spoken on the witness stand. We expect the Lord to keep His promises, and He expects us to keep ours. Truth is the cement that holds society together.

A second truth is the importance of authority and subordination in society and in the home. While all people are created equal before God and the Law, there are still levels of authority and responsibility that must be respected (Eph. 5:18-6:9). The unmarried maiden in her father's home is subject to her father's will, and the married woman is subject to her husband's will. Before making vows, the maiden should consult her father and the wife her husband, and the engaged maiden should speak with her betrothed. Relationships bring responsibilities, and to rush into unwise commitments is to incur penalties that can be costly. See Proverbs 20:25 and Ecclesiastes 5:1-6.

2. The victory of faith (Num. 31:1-54)

Though the people of Israel were wrong in getting entangled with the Midianites at Baal Peor, Midian was wrong in following Balaam's counsel and trying to destroy Israel. Those who curse Israel, God will curse (Gen. 12:1-3), and the time had come for God to punish Midian (25:16-18).[1] This battle would be a "dress rehearsal" for the battles Israel would fight in the land of Canaan. But this would be Moses' last battle; then he would meet "the last enemy" which is death (1 Cor. 15:26).

The battle (Num. 31:1-10). This battle was part of a "holy war" that Jehovah had declared against Midian because Midian had led Israel into sin. Certainly Israel was responsible for disobeying God and engaging in idolatry and immorality, and God punished them for it, but Midian was the chief offender, and such offenses must be punished (Matt. 18:7). The church has no mandate from God to engage in "holy wars" (John 18:10-11, 36) because our enemies aren't flesh and blood (Eph. 6:10ff) and our weapons are spiritual (2 Cor. 10:1-6). The sword of the Spirit is the only sword we use to advance the cause of Christ (Eph. 6:17-18).

We see here a pattern for the military engagements Israel would experience in Canaan: Israel received their instructions from God and trusted God to go before them and give them victory. We assume that Joshua led the army, but Phinehas, the son of the high priest, was also there with the priests who carried the ark of the covenant and blew the trumpets (Num.10:1-10). It was Phinehas who had demonstrated great courage and devotion to God when the sin of Baal Peor invaded the camp of Israel (25:7-15).

It was a monumental victory from the Lord, for all the Midianite men were killed but not a single Jewish soldier died in the conflict (31:7, 48-49). Many enemy leaders were killed during the battle, and after the battle Joshua killed five remaining Midianite kings, including Zur, the father of Cozbi, the woman with whom Zimri had sinned in the camp of Israel (25:14-15). Balaam, the architect of the great seduction at Baal Peor, was also killed (31:8, 16). Israel burned the cities and claimed the Midianite territory, later giving it to the tribe of Reuben (Josh. 13:15-23).

The purification (Num. 31:12-24). In disobedience to God's command, the soldiers did not exterminate all the Midianites but brought the women and children back as captives. This angered Moses, for the presence of the Midianite women and girls in the camp only gave further opportunity for the sin that had almost destroyed Israel. The nation had won the battle but was now in danger of losing the victory, a mistake that God's people have made more than once down through the centuries.

Moses commanded that the male children be slain as well as the women and girls who were not virgins. The virgins remaining could be taken by the men to be servants.[2] Since the soldiers had been defiled in battle by touching dead bodies, they had to obey the law of cleansing (19:11-13), and Moses applied this same rule to the female captives who were now expected to obey Jewish law. The great amount of wealth that was taken from Midian also had to be purified, either by fire or by the water of cleansing, and it would take a week for this purification to be completed.

Whether in peace or in war, it was important to Israel that they maintain a holy relationship with the Lord. They had to make a difference between the clean and the unclean, and no compromise was permitted. This week-long period of purification would remind the 12,000 soldiers and the people in the camp that the nations they would face in Canaan were dangerous, not only because they were enemies but they were also unclean sinners who could tempt them and defile them. Moses wanted to prevent another defeat like Baal Peor.

The spoils of battle (Num. 31:25-47). The people and animals that Israel took as spoils of war were distributed three ways: the soldiers got half, the people in the camp got half, and both the soldiers and the people gave a percentage to the Lord. After all, it was the Lord who gave them the victory. The soldiers were commanded to bring 1 person or animal out of 500, a total of 840; and the community was to bring 1 person or animal out of 50, which totaled 8,400. These animals and people were given to Eleazar the high priest to be used for the tabernacle ministry. The women were given tasks to perform to assist the priests and Levites (Ex. 38:8; 1 Sam. 2:22), from whom, we trust, they learned to know and obey the true and living God of Israel.

A special gift (Num. 31:48-54). Since there were only 12,000 men who attacked Midian (v. 5), there could have been 132 officers at the most who came to Moses with their special gifts to the Lord. However, it's possible that some commanders of 100 soldiers were in charge of more than one division. When the officers counted their men after the battle, they discovered that not one Israelite soldier had been lost! Only the Lord could have done such a miracle and the officers wanted to show their gratitude to Him. They brought a special gift for the sanctuary of God out of the spoils they themselves had received. It's one thing to bring offerings to God because it's our duty, and quite something else because we love Him and appreciate what He's done for us.

When the officers spoke of "making atonement" for themselves before the Lord (v. 50), they weren't suggesting that their gift of gold could in any way save their souls (Ps. 49:6-9; 1 Peter 1:18-19). According to Exodus 30:11-16, each time there was a census in Israel (and one had just occurred—Num. 26), the men twenty years and older were each to give a half shekel of silver as an offering to the Lord. This was known as "atonement money" and was originally used to make the sockets for the posts that helped to form the tabernacle frame (Ex. 38:21-28). Realizing that their lives had graciously been spared, the 12,000 soldiers wanted to give extra "atonement money" in thanksgiving to the Lord. Instead of bringing silver, they brought over 400 pounds of gold, which Moses and Eleazar received and put into the sanctuary.

3. The loyalty of people to each other (Num. 32:1-42)
A successful community or nation depends not only on keeping our word and trusting God for victory; it also depends on the loyalty of people to each other. Perhaps our word "patriotism" best describes this attitude, as long as we don't turn love of country into idolatry.[3]

The request (Num. 32:1-5). The tribes of Reuben and Gad were herdsmen and requested permission to settle east of the Jordan where the land was especially suited to pasturing flocks and herds. Half of the tribe of Manasseh would later join them (v. 33; Josh. 13:8ff). The Lord had given all that land into the hands of His people (Num. 21), so there was nothing to do but fortify it and occupy it. True, these tribes would be separated from the rest of the nation by the Jordan River, but they saw this as a minor concern.

Moses' reaction (Num 32:6-15). The great lawgiver may have reacted too quickly (Prov. 18:13), because his first thought was that these tribes were deserting the cause. Of course, their statement "Do not make us cross the Jordan" (Num. 32:5, NIV) would give Moses the impression that they were getting ready to settle down.

Moses always had the entire nation at heart as well as the great challenge of conquering and claiming the Promised Land. To Moses, it was a terrible sin for any of the tribes to retreat from conflict and fail to do their part in conquering the land. Just as the ten spies had discouraged the whole nation at Kadesh-Barnea, and led the people into thirty-eight wasted years, so these two tribes could discourage Israel by quitting at the very borders of their inheritance. More than that, their selfish attitude could arouse the anger of the Lord, and He might send judgment as He had done before when the people sinned. Even worse, He might just abandon the nation and let them die in the wilderness.

The tribes' defense (Num. 32:16-19). No doubt Reuben and Gad weren't too happy about being called "a brood of sinners" (v. 14, NIV), but it was their own fault for presenting their appeal in such a careless manner. Now they carefully explained to Moses that they were willing and prepared to enter the land and fight alongside their brothers until Canaan had been conquered. Only after the other tribes had received their inheritance would the two tribes (and later half of Manasseh) return to the Transjordan territory to settle down. However, first they would like to build fortified cities, to protect their wives and children, and pens for their cattle. Then they would join the other tribes in crossing the river and confronting the enemy.

The agreement (Num. 32:20-42). Moses repeated their promise to the Gadites and Reubenites and added a word of warning: If they didn't keep their promise, they would be sinning against the Lord, and their sin would catch up with them! The phrase "Be sure your sin will find you out" (v. 23) is often used in evangelistic appeals, and it can have that application; but the original intent was to admonish God's people. Their sin would be failure to keep their vow and unwillingness to assist their brothers and sisters in the task God had called them to do.

Moses wouldn't be alive when the nation crossed the river, so he called Eleazar, Joshua, and the leaders of the tribes and told them of the agreement. It would be their responsibility to see to it that the Transjordanic tribes kept their promise and crossed over the river to battle the nations in Canaan. The land they requested was theirs, but they would lose it if they didn't keep their promise.

The nation lingered long enough for the two and a half tribes to move into their land, defeat the enemies that remained, and get their families and flocks settled safely. But we can't help wondering if these Transjordanic tribes made a wise choice. They were outside the land of promise and separated from the rest of the nation. They made their choice only on the basis of personal gain: the land was good for their flocks and herds. Like Lot, they were walking by sight and not by faith (Gen. 13:10-11). The tribes did keep their promise, but in spite of that, their location across the Jordan created some problems (Josh. 22).

According to Hebrews 4, claiming the inheritance in the Promised Land is an illustration of the different ways believers today relate to the will of God and the inheritance He has for us now in Jesus Christ. Some people are like the older generation of Jews that perished in their wandering and never entered the land. Others are like the ten spies who visited the land and saw its wealth but failed to enter in. The Transjordanic tribes entered the land but didn't stay there. They preferred to live on the border and raise their cattle. God wants His people to be like the new generation that trusted God, entered the land, claimed the victory, and enjoyed the blessings.

4. The sovereignty of God (Num. 33:1-49)

The Lord commanded Moses to keep a list of the places Israel camped during their wilderness journey. Forty places are listed, starting with Rameses in Egypt (v. 3) and ending with the plains of Moab, across from Jericho (v. 49). Israel's exodus from Egypt is recorded in verses 3-4, and their march to and through the Red

Sea in verses 5-8. Verses 9-15 take Israel from Marah to Mount Sinai, and verses 16-36 from Sinai to Kadesh, where because of their unbelief Israel failed to enter the Promised Land. Their thirty-eight years of wandering fall between verses 36 and 37 and are graciously passed over in silence. The passage from Kadesh to the plains of Moab is recorded in verses 37-49.

But this chapter is more than a list of places; it's a testimony to the sovereignty of God in dealing with His people. As A.T. Pierson used to say, "History is His story." God doesn't just write history; He plans history and sees that His plan is executed. "The counsel of the Lord stands forever, the plans of His heart to all generations" (Ps. 33:11, NKJV). When Israel didn't permit God to rule, then He overruled. Israel lost the blessing but God achieved His purposes.

No difficulty was too great for God. He opened the Red Sea to let His people march through, and then He closed it and drowned the pursuing Egyptian army. When His people were in danger, God gave them victory over their enemies. When they were thirsty, He supplied water, and each morning He rained manna from heaven to feed them.

During this march, the older generation died off and the new generation took over. Miriam died at Kadesh (Num. 20:1) and another woman had to lead the choir. Aaron died at Mount Hor (vv. 23-29) and his son Eleazar became high priest. Before Moses died, he named Joshua as his successor. But in all these changes, God remained the same and never forsook His people. "Lord, Thou hast been our dwelling place in all generations" (Ps. 90:1).

The sovereignty of God doesn't destroy human individuality or responsibility. God is so great that He can will us the freedom to choose but still accomplish His purposes. What a mighty God is He! No wonder Paul wrote, "How unsearchable are His judgments, and His ways past finding out" (Rom. 11:33).

5. The certainty of the inheritance (Num. 33:50–35:34)
The land of Canaan is mentioned sixteen times in this passage, and the emphasis is on Israel entering the land and claiming the

promised inheritance. The Lord wanted the people to know that the thirty-eight year delay didn't alter His plans or annul His promises. The section opens with the Lord saying, "When you have crossed the Jordan into the land of Canaan" (33:51, NKJV). What an encouragement that statement was to them!

The inhabitants of the land (Num. 33:50-56). God wanted Israel's invasion of Canaan to be a total conquest. Israel was to drive out and dispossess the inhabitants, destroy the altars, images, and temples, and then divide the land among the tribes. The command was nothing new, because the Lord had told them this at Sinai (Ex. 23:20-33; 34:10-17). Moses would repeat it in his farewell message to the nation (Deut. 7; 12:1-3).

What were the reasons for the extermination of these nations? For one thing, this was God's judgment because of their wickedness (Gen. 15:15-16; Lev. 18:24-28). How they became so evil and what happened as a result is described in Romans 1:17-32. God had been long-suffering with them for centuries, but now it was time for judgment to fall.

A second reason was that the way might be cleared for the tribes of Israel to claim their inheritance (Num. 33:54). Just as a contractor must demolish buildings and clear land to make room for a new structure, so God had to wipe out the pagan societies in Canaan so that His people might move in and build a nation that would glorify God. The Promised Land would be the stage on which God would display His power, pour out His blessings, send His truth, and one day send His Son to die for the sins of the world.

A third reason for the extermination of the pagan nations was to remove temptation from the people of Israel who were prone to worship idols (vv. 55-56). During their wilderness march, the Jews revealed their appetite for the things of Egypt, and at Baal Peor, they succumbed to the seductions of Baal worship. If the pagan shrines were left standing, it wouldn't take long for Israel to forsake the Lord and start worshiping idols. Unfortunately, Israel didn't obey God's orders and ended up being snared by the practices of the heathen peoples left in the land (Jud. 2:6-15).

The boundaries of the land (Num. 34:1-15). In ancient days, there were no survey crews with scientific instruments for determining property lines. People cited towns and geographical features when they wanted to define boundaries. The Lord started with the south boundary of Canaan (vv. 3-5), then moved to the western border, which was the Mediterranean Sea (v. 6). Next came the north border (vv. 7-9), the east border (vv. 10-13), and the portion for the Transjordanic tribes (vv. 14-15).

The Lord gave His people a large land and a good land, but they didn't defeat their enemies and claim it all by faith (Josh. 15:63; 16:10; 17:11-13; Jud. 1:21-35).[4] Their eastern border didn't reach to the Mediterranean, for the Philistines still held that territory; nor did they get as far as Hamath on the north. On the east side of the Jordan, as you traveled north from the border of Manasseh, you would discover pockets of resistance in cities that Israel didn't conquer and destroy. Moses' prediction came true: the Canaanites became barbs in their eyes and thorns in their sides and led some of the Jews into sin (Num. 33:55).

Before we pass judgment on ancient Israel, what about the church today? Have we claimed by faith all that we have in Christ? Are there still pockets of resistance in our lives that draw us away from the Lord? "Let us therefore be diligent to enter that rest, lest anyone fall after the same example of disobedience" (Heb. 4:11, NKJV).

The dividing of the land (Num. 34:16-29). At the beginning of Numbers, Moses had a committee of twelve leaders to assist him in taking the census (1:5-16), and now he appointed a committee of ten leaders to help Joshua and Eleazar divide the land for the tribes living east of the Jordan (Josh. 14:1-19:51).

The cities in the land (Num. 35:1-34). After their conquest of Canaan, the Jews changed the names of many of the cities, and they also established forty-eight cities for the Levites to dwell in, and six cities of refuge (vv. 1-8). As we have seen, the Levites were scattered throughout Israel so they could minister to the people and teach them God's Law (Josh. 21). They were also granted pasture lands adjacent to the cities where they could care

141

for their flocks and herds.

The six cities of refuge were Kedesh, Shechem, and Hebron on the west side of the Jordan, and Golen, Ramoth, and Bezer on the east side. If you look at a map of ancient Israel, you will see that these cities were so located in the land that nobody would be too far away from an appointed city who needed to flee for refuge.

The nation of Israel had an army, but it didn't have anything equivalent to our modern police system. If somebody was murdered, the members of the family and clan saw to it that the murderer was punished. However, if a man accidentally killed someone, that was a case of manslaughter, not murder; and it would have been wrong to make him pay with his life.

The man could flee to one of the cities of refuge and present his case to the elders who would hear him and the witnesses. If they thought he was guilty of murder, they would turn him over to the family and the authorities for punishment. If they concluded that he was innocent, they allowed him to stay in the city of refuge under their protection until the death of the high priest. Then he was free to return home. He was not allowed to pay a ransom and be freed sooner (v. 32).

If the man was guilty, he was stoned to death. Murder was a capital crime in Israel for which there was no ransom (v. 32). The blood of innocent victims polluted the land, and the land belongs to the Lord (vv. 33-34; see Gen. 4:10; 9:5). The only way the land could be cleansed was by the death of the murderer.

Guilty sinners today can flee by faith to Jesus Christ and find refuge from the judgment of God (Heb. 6:18). Because Jesus is the ever-living High Priest, salvation is secure forever; for "He ever lives to make intercession for them" (7:25, NKJV). He bore the guily sinner's punishment; therefore, there can be no condemnation (Rom. 8:1).

THIRTEEN

SUMMARY AND REVIEW

The Wilderness School

The Jewish scholar Martin Buber once wrote, "All life is meeting." It's a brief statement, but the more you ponder it, the more luminous it becomes.

Life is meeting new circumstances, many of which we don't expect and can't control. Life is meeting new people and developing new relationships; it's meeting new ideas, some of which may upset us. As much as we try to avoid it, life is meeting ourselves and not always liking what we see. But most of all, life is meeting God, for He's always there, protecting us, wanting to teach, and always seeking to mature us.

Life is meeting, and meeting ought to lead to learning and learning to growing. Let's review some of the lessons we can learn while marching with Moses and the people of Israel, people just like you and me.

1. We learn about life

The metaphors for life are many, and each one teaches us something important. Sometimes life is like a battle and sometimes it's more like a race, but always it's a school where we need to be awake and alert to what God is trying to teach us. To Moses and the people of Israel, life was a journey, but a very special journey: from bondage to freedom, from childishness to maturity, from selfishness to service, from glorifying the past to anticipating the future.

From God's point of view, there are only three locations in this journey: Egypt, the place of bondage that seems like security; Canaan, the place of inheritance where God wants to give us His best; the wilderness, the place of unbelief, discipline, and falling short of the good things God has planned for us. This truth is elaborated in Hebrews 1–5.

Living the Christian life begins with deliverance from Egypt (bondage) through the grace and power of God. This we experience when we trust Jesus Christ, the Lamb of God, and commit our lives to Him. *But the essence of Christian living is to enter into your spiritual inheritance as quickly as possible.* When you reach the Kadesh-Barnea place in life, and all believers do, trust His Word and enter into your inheritance by faith. Don't worry about the giants, the enemy, the walled cities, or your own weakness and insignificance. Say with Caleb and Joshua, "The Lord is with us; fear them not" (Num. 14:9). "For we who have believed do enter into rest" (Heb. 4:3).

Before Israel arrived at Kadesh-Barnea, God put them through various trials because a certain amount of wilderness experience is good for people who want to grow (James 1:2-8; 1 Peter 1:3-9). *But the Lord doesn't want us to stay in the wilderness constantly.* Yes, there are lessons to learn, but there are even greater lessons to learn after we have claimed our inheritance in Christ. The Lord knows what trials we need, when we need them, and how long we need them; He always teaches those who are willing to learn.

Above all else, in the journey of life, we must be sure to follow the Lord as He goes before us, and we must not look back or hunger for the old life in Egypt. "Oh, taste and see that the Lord is good; blessed is the man who trusts in Him!" (Ps. 34:8, NKJV)

2. We learn about God

Israel repeatedly committed the same three mistakes that caused them no end of trouble: (1) they looked back and glorified Egypt; (2) they looked around and complained about their circumstances; and (3) they looked within and magnified their own desires. What they should have done was to look up to Almighty God and trust Him to see them through. We never learn the lessons we should learn if we plan the curriculum and write the textbook. We must leave it all with the Lord.

God's desire is that we develop character and become more like Jesus Christ. That's why He arranges the experiences of life and causes them to work together for our good and His glory (Rom. 8:27-29). We can't grow in grace unless we grow in the knowledge of God as revealed in Jesus Christ (2 Peter 3:18).

How do we learn about God? Primarily, we learn about God from His Word, both in private meditation and public worship. We also learn about God from personal experience, our own as well as that of others who share with us what He has done for them. In the difficult places of life, the Holy Spirit helps us recall and apply the truths of the Word. This ministry gives us wisdom to understand the situation better and faith to trust the promises we need to carry us through.

During their wilderness journey, Israel learned that God loved them and cared for them, but they didn't always believe it. "What shall we eat? What shall we drink?" were the repeated questions the Jews asked (Matt. 6:25-34), when they should have been saying to one another, "The Lord is our shepherd. We shall not lack for anything."

Israel also learned that God was long-suffering with them but wouldn't permit them to sin successfully. He was willing to forgive when they cried out to Him, but too often they didn't cry out in confession until first they cried out in pain. "For whom the Lord loves He corrects, just as a father the son in whom he delights" (Prov. 3:12, NKJV; see Heb. 12:1-11). How much pain we would avoid if only we submitted to the will of our loving Heavenly Father!

On life's journey, we learn that the Lord is the God of new beginnings. As Dr. V. Raymond Edman used to remind the students at Wheaton College, "It's always too soon to quit." It's sad that the Israelites doubted and disobeyed God so many times, but it's encouraging that God gave them a new start and encouraged them to keep moving toward their inheritance. True, a whole generation had to die before the nation could enter the Promised Land, but they died because of their own rebellion. In His grace, God forgave them; in His government, He permitted them to suffer the consequences of their sin. You can't negotiate the will of God. You either obey it, ignore it, or resist it.

One of the tests of spiritual maturity is what Paul called "increasing in the knowledge of God" (Col. 1:10). Not just in the knowledge of the Bible or Christian theology, but the knowledge of God Himself, His character, how He works, and how we can delight His heart. Moses grew in his understanding of God, but Israel failed to learn this lesson. "He made known His ways unto Moses, His acts unto the children of Israel" (Ps. 103:7). The Jews *saw* what God did, but Moses understood *why* God did it. There's a difference.

3. We learn about ourselves

As I studied the Book of Numbers in preparation for writing this book, I frequently said out loud, "How could they do that? Don't they realize what they're doing?" Then I would pause and confess, "But, Lord, I've done the same thing. Forgive me." People are people, whether marching slowly through an ancient wilderness or driving at high speed down a modern freeway. "For He knows our frame; He remembers that we are dust" (Ps. 103:14, NKJV).

Socrates said that the unexamined life was not worth living, but most people don't like to face the truth about themselves. Like our first parents, we run and hide and defend ourselves by making excuses and blaming others. Not many people pray as honestly as David did in Psalm 51.

One of the first lessons we learn about ourselves from Israel's experience is that all of us have a fallen nature that's prone to resist the will of God, and the sooner we admit it, the easier it will be to make the journey. Peter acknowledged that he was a sinful man (Luke 5:8), and Paul confessed, "I know that in me...nothing good dwells" (Rom. 7:18, NKJV). Our Lord warned us, "The spirit indeed is willing, but the flesh is weak" (Matt. 26:41).

Another lesson we learn about ourselves is that we don't enjoy changes in our lives and the discomfort they usually bring. One day the people were thirsty; the next day they were attacked by an enemy; for forty days, they wondered what had happened to their leader. All of us want life to be one vast comfort zone where we're sheltered from change, all the while forgetting that God-ordained change can be used to mold our character and help us grow up.

If there's one lesson the Jews frequently failed to learn it was that complaining and criticizing are sins that God judges. When we complain to God about our lot in life, we not only commit the sin of ingratitude, but we also reveal pride (we think we know more than God knows, and why should this happen to us!), unbelief (we don't really trust Him), and impatience. If we would learn to trust God, praise Him for His mercies, and wait for Him to accomplish His will, we'd grow a lot faster and experience a lot less misery.

One last lesson from Israel's experiences: age is no guarantee of maturity. It's possible to grow old and not grow up. When the nation failed at Kadesh-Barnea, the fault didn't lie with the young people but with the older people. To prove it, God rejected the older generation (twenty years and older), gave it time to die off, and then made a new beginning with the younger generation.

The church needs both the older saints and the younger ones, because each generation has something to contribute, and we can all learn from each other (Titus 2:1-8). But Moses was wise to train Joshua to be his successor, and Paul was wise to equip Timothy to succeed him in Ephesus.

4. We learn about faith

Life is a journey that we make by faith, for only God knows the end from the beginning. Actually, everybody lives by faith in someone or something. The difference between Christians and non-Christians is the *object of that faith*. Christians put their faith in God and His Word, while non-Christians trust themselves, their experience, and ability, their money, and perhaps their friends. But Israel had the bad habit of walking by sight, not by faith, and it was this failure to trust God that caused the nation so much trouble.

No sooner had the Lord delivered the people from Egypt than they stood by the Red Sea trembling with fear and wanting to go back. Why? Because they didn't really believe that the God who had redeemed them could finish the task and see them through. But when God begins a work, He completes it (Phil. 1:6).

Faith is not believing in spite of evidence; that's superstition. Faith is obeying God in spite of what we see or hear, how we feel, or what might happen. The Jews had been given all the evidence they needed that God was concerned about them and had the power to deliver them, protect them, and take them to the Promised Land. The devastation of the land of Egypt was proof of God's power, so why should the nation not trust Him?

Years ago, I heard Vance Havner give a message on Hebrews 11 that has stayed in my heart and encouraged me in many a difficult hour. This was his outline:

Faith chooses the imperishable (Heb. 11:24-26)
Faith sees the invisible (Heb. 11:27)
Faith does the impossible (Heb. 11:28-29)

Once we've made that choice to follow the Lord and live for eternal values, the rest is bound to follow: He will help us see the invisible and do the impossible, no matter what the circumstances may be around us.

Faith must be nourished if it's to grow strong, and that's where the Scriptures come in, for "faith comes by hearing, and hearing by the word of God" (Rom. 10:17, NKJV). When Moses declared God's Word, Israel didn't really hear it or mix it with faith, so their faith didn't grow (Heb. 4:1-2). Faith is like the muscles in your arms: If you don't exercise them, they lose their strength. Every trial of life is an opportunity to claim God's promises and trust Him for the solution.

5. We learn the importance of one believer

Numbers is a book of "counting." Twice Moses counted the men available to serve in the army, and he also counted the Levites. Somebody even counted the number of people who died in the various plagues God sent to discipline them. Those ancient Jews would be shocked to see how much counting goes on in today's world, most of it done unannounced by electronic devices.

God wants all of His children to be the kind He can count on. The Lord could count on Moses and Aaron to lead the people in His will, even though they each disappointed the Lord on a couple of occasions. Joshua and Caleb were men God could count on, and so were Eleazar and his son Phinehas. Anybody can be a statistic, a number in a record, but it takes faith and courage to be the kind of person the Lord can count on.

We have a choice. We can go with the unbelieving majority and miss God's very best, complaining our way through life, or we can stand with the minority and dare to believe God and follow His commands. We can crave comfort or respond to challenge. We can look back and yearn for carnal security or look ahead and eagerly anticipate spiritual maturity. We can wander in the wilderness of unbelief, selfishness, and disobedience or enter into the Promised Land with its battles and trials, trusting God to give us the victory.

"He shall choose our inheritance for us" (Ps. 47:4).

Will we choose to claim our inheritance and use it for His glory? Will we be counted among the conquerors?

Chapter One

Order in the Camp
(Numbers 1–4; 9:1-14)

1. What does Wiersbe mean when he exhorts us to "Be Counted"?

2. What three things can studying the Book of Numbers help us to understand?

3. What were the stages in Moses' preparation for conquest?

4. Why was the Passover bread to be made without yeast? What was the significance of the bitter herbs?

5. The Book of Numbers records 150 occurrences of God speaking to Moses. How does God speak to you today?

6. Israel had physical enemies and battles to fight. How are Christians to fight today? What kind of warfare do we use, and who is our enemy? (Eph. 6:10-12)

7. How are worship and warfare related?

8. In what way can Israel's camp be an example for the church today?

9. Why is it important that we know so much about the ministry of the Levites?

10. What two qualities does Wiersbe say are essential for the camp and for successful warfare?

Chapter Two
Dedication and Celebration—Part I
(Numbers 5-7)

1. How can Christians sometimes be their own biggest obstacle to evangelism?

2. What is the basic purpose of God's emphasis on clean and unclean?

3. What was the significance of the interpersonal laws concerning confession and restitution?

4. What is the main message of the adultery test?

5. Why would men or women take on the Nazirite vow?

6. When, if ever, is it proper today to make a vow to the Lord? When is it not proper?

7. In what ways can you show your total dedication to the Lord?

8. When you read or hear Aaron's blessing, which images especially touch you?

9. What encouragement and what challenge can we draw from the long account of the offerings of the leaders?

10. What special offering could you bring to the Lord?

Chapter Three

Dedication and Celebration—Part II
(Numbers 8:1-10:10)

1. God spoke to Moses face-to-face. When will we see the Lord face-to-face? (1 Cor. 13:12)

2. Where was the lampstand placed? What was its practical significance? Of what did the lampstand remind the priests? What does the oil for the lamp symbolize?

3. How can believers today "shine their light"?

4. What were the responsibilities of the Levites? How were they set apart? How do people get chosen and ready for spiritual service?

5. When we feel competitive, prideful, or shameful in our spiritual service, what should we remember?

6. How is serving the Lord related to serving His people?

7. What does Wiersbe say is "vitally important to a fulfilled and fruitful Christian life"?

8. How do the pillars of cloud and fire symbolize the Word of God?

9. What does it mean to "walk in the darkness" and to "walk in the light"?

10. What were the purposes of the trumpets in the life of God's people in the past? What will the trumpet's purpose be in the future?

Chapter Four

Marching to Moab
(Numbers 10:11–12:16)

1. Israel had been comfortable at Sinai but God soon said to move on. In what area of your life are you comfortable but you sense that God is telling you to move on?

2. Why is complacency the enemy of spiritual growth?

3. What do you think about Moses' decision to ask Hobab to be Israel's "eyes" in the wilderness? Did this indicate a lack of trust in the Lord? Why or why not?

4. Moses invited others to come with Israel and enjoy God's blessings. Who could you invite to share in God's blessings? How will you do this?

5. What was the purpose of Moses' prayers each time they stopped or started on their journey?

6. Who were the "mixed multitude"? What negative effect did they have on the Israelite community?

7. Why are the counterfeits inside the church more damaging than the enemies outside the church?

8. Why did Moses become discouraged? In his despair and frustration, what did he ask God to do? How did God respond to Moses' complaint of "I can't do it"?

9. Where did Miriam and Aaron go wrong?

10. What evidence is recorded of the meekness of Moses?

Chapter Five

Crisis at Kadesh
(Numbers 13–14)

1. What does Canaan represent for us?

2. What were five of the sins Israel committed at Kadesh?

3. In what way did the Israelites show they doubted God's Word? When do you find yourself most tempted to doubt God's Word?

4. When have you seen discouragement spread because of unbelief? Why is unbelief so serious?

5. What does a complaining spirit give evidence of?

6. Wiersbe says that "the will of God is the expression of the love of God for His people." How have you seen this proved true in your own life?

7. What were Moses' four reasons for God to spare the Israelites?

8. In what ways do children suffer for the sins of parents or grandparents?

9. What is the difference between regret and true repentance? Between admitting sin and confessing sin?

10. After studying the episode at Kadesh-Barnea, how would you define "faith" in this context?

Chapter Six

A Question of Authority
(Numbers 15–17)

1. What four special instructions did Moses give the new generation? What did their enjoyment of the land depend on?

2. What does the fine flour given in sacrifice picture?

3. The drink offering can symbolize life poured out for God. How, practically speaking, can you pour out your life for God?

4. What different types of sins did the sacrifices cover? For what one type of sin was there no sacrifice?

5. What was the purpose of wearing the tassels? What creative reminder can help you to remember to obey God's law?

6. What is usually behind complaining and rebelling?

7. What was Moses' response to Korah's rebellion? In what situations would this example be helpful to you?

8. Why do you think people so often do not learn from history?

9. What should be our proper attitude toward our church leaders today? When, if ever, would it be right to remove a church leader from a position of responsibility?

10. What has the Lord given believers for encouragement?

Chapter Seven

Another Crisis at Kadesh
(Numbers 18–20)

1. Why was the priesthood God's gift to Israel?

2. What are the commonalities and differences between the priest/Levite distinction and the elder/deacon distinction?

3. How were the priests and Levites cared for? How can and should we care for our church leaders, both paid and unpaid?

4. What do you think is the Christian's responsibility in the area of giving?

5. How do you understand the change from the Old Testament teaching "clean" and "unclean" to the New Testament teaching of Paul that "nothing is unclean of itself"? (Rom. 14:14)

6. In what way are God's people now to cleanse themselves?

7. How can the account of Moses getting water from a rock encourage you in difficult times?

8. Moses was disciplined by the Lord for disobedience. How can we know if at any certain point we are being disciplined by the Lord?

9. Why did Moses decide that Israel wouldn't go through Edom but would instead take a new route?

10. Why are new beginnings a normal part of victorious Christian service?

Chapter Eight

Marching in Victory—and Defeat
(Numbers 21)

1. How would you answer the objection that Christianity is boring?

2. What did it mean to "utterly destroy" a city or a people? Why was it approved of, and even commanded, that the Israelites utterly destroy whole cities?

3. How can believers be helped to "walk and not faint"?

4. In their difficulties, the Israelites forgot God's promise and the "big picture." When you encounter obstacles, what can you do to remember God's promise and the "big picture"?

5. In what ways was the manna a type of Jesus Christ and of the Word of God?

6. Looking up at the bronze serpent brought healing to the dying people. How does Jesus use this event to help us understand God's grace? Of those bitten by the fiery serpents, who could not be delivered from death?

7. The Israelites were grateful for the well God provided. Why were they so grateful for water? What are you especially grateful for today?

8. How do you see God's plan unfold in Sihon's attack on Israel?

9. Wiersbe warns against borrowing "secular words" to express praise and worship to God. What does he mean? Why might it be acceptable to borrow tunes and not words?

10. What was the pattern to the conquests of Israel in the land of Canaan? When could you use this same pattern?

Chapter Nine

Principalities and Powers—Part I
(Numbers 22:1–23:26)

1. What does the church today battle against? Why do we lose sight of our true enemy?

2. Balaam's words in Numbers 22:18 sound great. Do you think it was sincere or just pious talk? How can we know if a person is sincere?

3. Since the Lord had given his permission for Balaam to go with the men, why was the Lord so angry with Balaam for going?

4. If God would use Balaam to speak God's word, what other types of people might we find God using to accomplish His will?

5. What truths about the people of Israel did God's message to Balaam reveal?

6. What role, if any, does "imitation" of the world have in outreach?

7. In what ways are God's people to be separate from the world? How do you work this out in your life?

8. Why is the love of money so destructive?

9. Why do you think God did not allow Balaam to speak false prophecies, even though He allowed other false prophets in other situations?

10. What did the first two oracles of Balaam picture?

Chapter Ten

Principalities and Powers—Part II
(Numbers 23:27-25:18)

1. What did the third oracle of Balaam emphasize?

2. How could Balaam have such a powerful experience of the Lord and still not have saving faith? What can we learn from this?

3. What comfort can a believer draw from Numbers 24:23, "Alas, who can live except God has ordained it"?

4. God did not allow Balaam to curse Israel. But after Balaam blessed them, what did he do? What did Balaam appeal to in the Israelites to get them to stumble?

5. What did the Israelites look to Baal for? Why should they have known better?

6. In 2 Peter 2, how are dangerous false teachers compared to Balaam?

7. How can God work out His plan when people reject God's rule over their lives?

8. When are we walking in "the way of Balaam"? What was Balaam's tragic error?

9. What were the sins of the Israelites at Baal Peor? How could they rationalize this "doctrine of Balaam"?

10. How can we be careful to avoid being religious and yet "rotten at the heart"?

Chapter Eleven

A New Beginning
Numbers 26–29; 36)

1. What four important responsibilities did Moses fulfill in preparation for Israel's conquering future?

2. How did the tribes react to the inheritance given them? What parallels can you draw between this and how believers might react to situations God has put them in?

3. How did Moses respond when approached by the five daughters of Zelophehad for an unprecedented inheritance question? What do we see of God's view of women in this change of policy?

4. What experiences and qualities in Joshua made him a great choice for Moses' successor?

5. What two ingredients were crucial for Israel's success?

6. What does it mean to be a living sacrifice? What spiritual sacrifices can we bring to God?

7. What happened at Pentecost? What difference does this make?

8. What did the holy Day of Atonement picture? What did the Feast of Tabernacles look forward to?

9. What three lessons can believers learn from these accounts of offerings?

10. How is Jesus Christ our high priest?

Chapter Twelve

Preparing for Conquest
(Numbers 30-35)

1. What is the difference between a vow and an oath? What is the basic principle concerning vows for men? for women?

2. Why is speech so powerful? Why is speaking truth and keeping your word so essential?

3. Could there ever be a "holy war" now? Why or why not?

4. What was the reason for the week of purification after the defeat of Midian?

5. What kind of offering could you make out of special gratitude to the Lord?

6. Why did the two and a half tribes decide to settle outside of the Promised Land? Why weren't these very good reasons?

7. What evidences of God's sovereignty do you see from the time of the Exodus from Egypt to the beginning of conquest in the Promised Land?

8. How does God's sovereignty work together with individual responsibility?

9. Why did the resident nations in the Promised Land need to be exterminated?

10. Cities of refuge were provided for the people of Israel. What refuge is provided for believers today?

Chapter Thirteen
The Wilderness School
(Summary and Review)

1. What does Wiersbe say is the "essence of Christian living"? What does this mean?

2. What three mistakes did Israel continually make?

3. Why does God allow trials in our life? What is God's desire for us?

4. What did Israel learn about God during their wilderness journey?

5. What does it mean to you that "the Lord is the God of new beginnings"?

6. One test of spiritual maturity is what Paul calls "increasing in the knowledge of God" (Col. 1:10). How can we assess our growth in this area?

7. What do we learn about ourselves from Israel's experience as recorded in the Book of Numbers?

8. What must be coupled with age to have true maturity?

9. What is the difference between the faith of Christians and that of non-Christians? What is faith? How is faith nourished?

10. What kind of person can the Lord count on? What are some choices we have to make as we decide how to live our life?

NOTES

Chapter 1

1. Samuel Eliot Morison, *The Oxford History of the American People* (New York: Oxford University Press, 1965), 1030.

2. The Jews also call Numbers *bemidbar*, "in the wilderness."

3. The phrase, "by their polls" in the KJV (vv. 2, 18) means "by their heads," that is, one by one. The modern "poll tax" means "head tax." In ancient times, men "polled" their heads, i.e., thinned out their hair (2 Sam. 14:26).

4. Leviticus 16:12 suggests that the two sons of Aaron may have been intoxicated when they brought "false fire" into the sanctuary. What they did stemmed from pride because they were disobeying God's clear instructions. At the beginning of Israel's formal worship at the tabernacle, this divine judgment made it clear to priests and people alike that only what God authorized must be practiced there. Innovations were not permitted.

5. When you add the numbers recorded in 3:22, 28, and 34, you get a total of 22,300, but the total in verse 39 is 22,000. What happened to the other 300 Levites? Some Hebrew texts of verse 28 read 8,300 instead of 8,600, and this would make the difference. The Hebrew language uses letters for numbers and it would be easy for a copyist to make an error.

6. It seems odd that the laver isn't mentioned in this list of furnishings, for surely it had to be carried in the wilderness march. This is only one peculiar thing about it. Another is that no dimensions are given for the laver, so we don't know its size or shape. The laver is commonly thought to be circular, but there's no Scripture to support this. The Hebrew word translated "laver" in Exodus 30:18 etc. is translated "scaffold" ("platform," NIV) in 2 Chronicles 6:13, and it's clear that its shape was square. The laver could have been a square container, perhaps the same shape as the altar of burnt offering; and they may have been carried together.

7. The word translated "burden" in Galatians 6:5 means "a soldier's

pack," and every soldier has to carry his own pack. If my car breaks down, my neighbor can help me by driving my children to school, but my neighbor can't assume my parental responsibilities in the home so that I can do as I please. There are some burdens that you have to shoulder and can't hand to others.

Chapter 2

1. This admonition is repeated in Leviticus 19:2; 20:7, 26; 21:8; and 1 Peter 1:15-16.

2. When you compare verses 16, 18-19, 21, 24 and 26, you get the impression that certain actions were performed twice, but this isn't the case. But verse 24 only states that the priest will give her the water, while verse 26 says that the woman drinks it. Verse 16 states the intent of the husband to "stand before the Lord," while verse 18 describes the official action of the priest. In verse 19, the priest puts her under oath, while in verse 21 he announces the curses attached to the oath.

3. According to the NIV, the judgment for her sin was that her abdomen would swell and her thigh waste away (vv. 21, 27). The margin reads "have a miscarrying womb and barrenness," both of which would make her childless. These judgments imply that, after the trial, the guilty wife and her suspicious husband continued normal marriage relations; otherwise, how could she conceive and miscarry or demonstrate that her womb was barren?

4. I'm not overlooking the fact that the husband's motive may be very noble, i.e., removing sin from the holy camp of Israel. But the woman wasn't stoned and the sinner removed from the camp. She continued to live in the camp, although bearing the pain of her sin.

5. Matthew 2:23 states that our Lord's title "Nazarene" was given to Him in fulfillment of what the prophets wrote, but we can find no such prophecy in the Old Testament. However, the prophets did announce that Messiah would be poor and rejected and bear reproach, and Nazareth was a city that was despised and scorned by many. When Jesus was connected with Nazareth, and even took the city's name to the shameful cross (John 19:19), He was bearing the reproach of sinners and identifying Himself with the despised and rejected of mankind.

6. For the spiritual significance of the Jewish sacrifices to believers today, see my book on Leviticus, *Be Holy*, published by Chariot Victor.

7. Nowhere in Scripture is wine condemned simply because it is wine. The Jews considered wine a gift and blessing from God (Ps. 104:13-15; Jud. 9:13). However, the Bible clearly condemns drunkenness (Deut. 21:20-21; Prov. 20:1; 23:20-21, 29-35; Isa. 5:11, 22; Hab. 2:15-16; Luke 21:34; Rom. 13:13-14; 1 Cor. 5:11; Eph. 5:18; 1 Peter 4:3-5).

Chapter 3

1. It's unfortunate that the phrase "the priesthood of the believer" has become so popular, because it ought to be "the priesthood of believers." It's not only that I am "a royal priest" but that I belong to a "royal priesthood." The exercising of priestly duties and privileges is a collective activity on the part of the church. Nadab and Abihu acted independently of the other priests and were slain because of their pride (Lev. 10).

2. For details about the tabernacle, see Exodus 25–31, and for an exposition of the significance of these furnishings, see my book *Be Delivered*, published by Chariot Victor.

3. The people provided the materials out of which the tabernacle was constructed (Ex. 25:1-8; 35:4–36:7) and also the oil for the lamps. It's likely that they also brought the flour which was used to bake the twelve loaves of bread (Lev. 24:1-9).

4. It's likely that the shaving and washing of clothes took place after the rest of the ceremony was completed. Otherwise Moses and Aaron would have to delay the ceremony a long time while 22,000 men had their bodies shaved and their clothes washed and dried, all of which demanded privacy.

5. When David organized the priests and Levites in preparation for their enlarged ministry in the temple, he lowered the age of entering service to twenty (1 Chron. 23:24, 27), apparently at the Lord's direction (28:11-19).

6. Nehemiah 9:20 adds that God's Spirit instructed the people through the Word that God gave through Moses, and that Law covered most of the matters related to everyday life. No Jew ever had to seek

God's will as to what he should eat, because the Law told him what foods were clean and unclean. For most of the decisions God's people have to make today, we can turn to the Word of God and find precepts, principles, and promises that will guide us. In matters where we are perplexed, God will guide us if we sincerely want His will (John 7:17) and seek His will with all our heart.

7. These trumpets must not be confused with the rams' horn trumpets (shophar) that were used at Jericho (Josh. 6:20) and at Gideon's battle against Midian (Jud. 7:16-22), and that are used today in sacred services in Jewish synagogues.

8. In David's day, the number of trumpeters had increased to seven, and they blew their trumpets before the ark of God (1 Chron. 15:24). When Solomon brought the ark into the temple, there were 120 priests blowing trumpets as an act of worship (2 Chron. 5:12).

Chapter 4

1. It wasn't unusual in that time and place for people to have more than one name. Some think that Reuel was his given name and Jethro his official title as a priest. Jethro means "excellence."

2. Charles H. Spurgeon, *The Metropolitan Tabernacle*, vol. 7, 161.

3. Some Bible students feel that the cloud not only led Israel but also spread out over the people each day, sheltering them from the hot sun as they marched. The NIV translates verse 34, "The cloud of the Lord was over them by day when they set out from the camp." See Psalm 105:39 and 1 Corinthians 10:1.

4. David must have meditated on these words of Moses because he used some of them in the opening verse of Psalm 68. The psalm glorifies God for His wonderful work of delivering and guiding His people, and by faith David claimed God's help in conquering his own enemies.

5. Often at the beginning of a new era in salvation history, God judged sin in a dramatic way to warn His people. Other examples are Nadab and Abihu (Lev. 10), Achan (Josh. 7), Uzzah (2 Sam. 6:1-7), and Ananias and Sapphira (Acts 5).

6. While the Hebrew word used in Exodus 12:38 is different from the one in Numbers 11:4, the idea is the same: people of various races who were not Jewish and therefore not children of the covenant.

7. Some of God's greatest leaders had their times of discouragement, including Joshua (Josh. 7), Elijah (2 Kings 19), David (Ps. 42), Jeremiah (Jer. 12:1-4; 15:15-18), and Paul (2 Cor. 1:8-11).

8. Verse 25 doesn't suggest that Moses had "less of the Spirit" after this event than before. The Holy Spirit is a person and is spirit, and therefore is not divisible. God didn't "divide up" the Spirit among seventy-one men. He gave to the elders the same Spirit that empowered Moses.

9. It took only a brief time each morning to gather enough manna to sustain them for the day, but the Jews were willing to spend two days and a night getting meat to satisfy their carnal appetites. Unspiritual people in churches spend time, money, and energy on things that satisfy their own desires, but they would never make those sacrifices just to please God and do His will.

10. Miriam is one of ten women in Scripture who were called prophetesses: Deborah (Jud. 4:4), Huldah (2 Kings 22:14), Noadiah (Neh. 6:14), Isaiah's wife (Isa. 8:3), Anna (Luke 2:36), and the four daughters of Philip the evangelist (Acts 21:9).

11. "Cush" in *The International Standard Bible Encyclopedia*, vol. 1, 839 (Grand Rapids: W.B. Eerdmans, 1979). Because of this fact, Moses' marriage has no relationship to the question of interracial marriages.

12. If Moses was a meek man, why did he tell us? Isn't this a sign of pride? The Hebrew root of the word translated "meek" is simply "to be bowed down." Some translate it "burdened," referring to all the troubles Moses had to carry (11:14). Others think that an inspired "editor" added this verse at a later date, but we have no evidence to prove it. In his writings, Moses was honest enough to record his sins and failures, and we accept what he wrote, so why can't we accept a statement about his godly character? Paul wrote in a similar way in 2 Corinthians 10:1, 11:5, and 12:11-12.

Chapter 5

1. The rabbis have noted ten times when the nation or individuals in the nation tested the Lord: at the Red Sea (Ex. 14:10-12); at Marah (15:22-24); when the manna was given (Ex. 16); when some of the Jews stored up the manna (vv. 19-20); when some of them looked for

manna on the Sabbath (vv. 27-30); when the people cried for water (17:1-7); when they worshiped the golden calf at Sinai (Ex. 32); when they complained (Num. 11:1-3); when they cried for flesh to eat (vv. 4ff); and when they rebelled at Kadesh-Barnea. However, the phrase "ten times" in 14:22 may simply mean "many times."

2. The KJV uses the word "carcasses" to describe the dead bodies of the Israelites (vv. 29, 32-33, 35), as though they were only animals being buried in the wilderness. But the Hebrew word simply means "dead bodies." When the KJV was translated, "carcass" meant the dead body of either a human or an animal, but since the middle of the eighteenth century, the word has been applied primarily to animals.

3. Some people say, "I have sinned," and really mean it, like Achan (Josh. 7:20), David (2 Sam. 12:13; Ps. 51:4; 1 Chron. 24:8, 17), and the Prodigal Son (Luke 15:18, 21); others are merely saying pious words, like Pharaoh (Ex. 9:27), Balaam (Num. 22:34), King Saul (1 Sam. 15:24, 30; 26:21), Shimei (2 Sam. 19:20), and Judas (Matt. 27:4). It takes more than words to exhibit true repentance.

4. It's helpful to read Joshua 1–5 and see how God prepared the new generation for entering the land and confronting the enemy. The men were circumcised as the covenant was renewed, and the nation celebrated Passover, remembering God's great victory over Egypt. The ark went before the people and God was glorified as they crossed the Jordan and entered the land. From start to finish, the entire enterprise was directed by God, and the people obeyed.

Chapter 6

1. Thirty-eight years later, Moses will rehearse the Law to the new generation in what we call the Book of Deuteronomy; he'll emphasize the fact that obedience brings life and blessing to the nation but disobedience brings death and cursing. Joshua will repeat this message after the nation enters Canaan and begins its conquest (Josh 8:30-35). These same principles apply to God's people today.

2. Of course, the offerings point to Jesus Christ (Heb. 10:1-18). He gave Himself completely on the cross (burnt offering) and paid for the sins of the world (sin offering, trespass offering). He is our peace and made peace on the cross (peace offering), and He is the satisfying bread

of life (meal offering). For a study of the levitical sacrifices, see *Be Holy* (Chariot Victor).

3. Fine flour would be the very best they had to offer. The Jews usually ate a coarse bread made from ordinary meal.

4. Wine is also connected with the Spirit in Acts 2:13 and Ephesians 5:18, but only by way of contrast. People who are drunk lose their self-control, but self-control is one of the fruit of the Spirit (Gal. 5:22-23). The hilarity of drunken people is foolish and embarrassing, but the joy of the Lord glorifies God and gives opportunity for witness.

5. Christ's prayer on the cross, "Father, forgive them; for they know not what they do" (Luke 23:34), did not automatically bring divine forgiveness to the Jewish nation or the people responsible for His death. But it did postpone the judgment that the nation deserved and finally received in A.D. 70. See Acts 3:17, and note Paul's testimony in 1 Timothy 1:13.

6. When David committed adultery with Bathsheba, it was a deliberate sin that defied God's will, and it was especially heinous because he was the king and not only knew the laws of God but had the responsibility of enforcing them. He could bring no sacrifice (Ps. 51:15), so he threw himself completely on the mercy of God. The Lord forgave him, but David had to suffer the painful consequences of his sin (2 Sam. 12:13-14).

7. Subordination doesn't imply inferiority. A buck private may have more character and wisdom than the general, but he's still a buck private who has to obey orders.

8. It seems that the sons of Korah were not a part of their father's rebellion because they become well-known musicians in Israel. "For [or by] the sons of Korah" is part of the heading of eleven psalms (Pss. 42; 44–49; 84–85; 87–88). They were important musicians in the tabernacle and temple worship.

9. Cain belonged to the devil (1 John 3:12), Balaam seduced Israel to indulge in sins of the flesh (Num. 25), and Korah acted like the people of the world in promoting himself and defying the will of God. Believers must constantly beware of temptations from the world, the flesh, and the devil (Eph. 2:1-3).

Chapter 7

1. The KJV and NIV both use the verb "join" to describe the Levites' relationship to the priests (vv. 2, 4). "Levi" means "joined" in Hebrew (Gen. 29:34).

2. The tribes of Simeon and Levi had a bad reputation for anger and cruelty because of the way they treated the Shechemites (Gen. 34), so Jacob prophesied that they would be scattered in Israel (Gen. 49:5-7). Simeon was absorbed into Judah (Josh. 19:1, 9) and the Levites were scattered to forty-eight locations across the land. However, this also gave many people the opportunity to learn the Law of God from their Levite neighbors.

3. For an exposition of these chapters about "grace giving," see my book *Be Encouraged* (Chariot Victor).

4. Abraham failed in his strength, which was his faith. David's strength was his integrity, and that's where he failed; Peter's strength was his courage, yet he wilted before the question of a young girl. Satan knows how to turn strength into weakness, but the Lord can turn weakness into strength.

5. This account should warn us against building our theology on events instead of on Scripture. The fact that God meets a need or blesses a ministry is no proof that the people involved are necessarily obeying the Lord in the way they minister.

6. However, Moses did make it into the land when he came with Elijah to see Jesus glorified on the Mount of Transfiguration (Matt. 17:1-8).

Chapter 8

1. We have a translation problem here. The KJV reads, "Israel came by way of the spies," that is, the route the twelve spies took forty years before (Num. 13). The NIV and NASB have transliterated the Hebrew word as "Atharim," assuming it is the name of a city.

2. This vow applied not only to Arad but to all the cities in Canaan. The Jews were commanded to utterly destroy the evil Canaanite culture (Ex. 23:20-33; Deut. 7), and they began with Arad, promising the Lord that they would obey His will. We don't have to make vows in order to receive God's help, but we must do God's will in God's way if

we expect to have His blessing. For a description of Israel's destruction of their enemies, see Joshua 10:16-43.

3. Their, "We have sinned," recorded in Numbers 14:40 couldn't have been a sincere confession because they were still rebelling against God and seeking to have their own way. The statement meant, "So we made a mistake, but we can rectify it." Had they truly been broken before God, they wouldn't have left the camp and tried to fight their way into Canaan.

4. Two other books no longer extant are The Book of Jasher (Josh. 10:13; 2 Sam. 1:18) and The Chronicles of the Kings of Israel and of Judah (1 Kings 14:19, 29).

5. In our Lord's synagogue sermon in John 6, note how many times He spoke of the bread "from heaven" and His coming down from heaven (vv. 32-33, 38, 50-51, 58). The Jews were struck by this claim (vv. 41-42).

6. During the time when Jephthah was judge, the Ammonites claimed that Israel illegally possessed their land, and they wanted it back. But Jephthah knew his history and reminded them of what really happened (Jud. 11:1-28).

7. Inspiration guarantees that what is written in the Scriptures is "God-breathed" and that the text is what God desires. What is recorded includes a variety of literature, including the lies of Satan and of men. Paul quoted from secular pagan writers (Acts 17:28; 1 Cor. 15:33; Titus 1:12), but this doesn't mean that these writers were inspired by God in what they wrote. It only means that the Spirit guided Luke as he wrote the Book of Acts so that what He recorded was what God wanted and therefore could be trusted.

8. Several hymns are sung to a Croatian melody adapted by Franz Joseph Haydn for a German patriotic song, including "Glorious Things of Thee Are Spoken," "Praise the Lord, Ye Heavens Adore Him," and "We Are Living, We Are Dwelling." The melody of "Joyful, Joyful We Adore Thee" is borrowed from Beethoven's Ninth Symphony. The Christmas song "What Child Is This" is usually song to the tune of "Greensleeves," an old English melody.

Chapter 9

1. It's unfortunate that "spiritual warfare" has been caricatured and discredited by some people as "chasing after demons." It's also unfortunate that some well-meaning people who believe in "spiritual warfare" have developed a theology not consistent with biblical teaching. For balanced biblical presentations, see *The Bondage Breaker* and *Released from Bondage* by Neil T. Anderson (Here's Life), *3 Crucial Questions about Spiritual Warfare* by Clinton E. Arnold (Baker), *The Adversary* and *Overcoming the Adversary* by Mark I. Bubeck (Moody), *Powers of Evil* by Sydney H.T. Page (Baker), *Spiritual Warfare* by Timothy Warner (Crossway), and *The Strategy of Satan* by Warren W. Wiersbe (Tyndale).

2. In the KJV, the Hebrew word translated "divination" (22:7; 23:23) and "soothsayer" (Josh. 13:22) with reference to Balaam also describes the occult practices of the witch of Endor (1 Sam. 28:8) and the work of the false prophets (Jer. 14:14; 2 Kings 17:17; Ezek. 13:6, 23). Balaam was not a prophet in the biblical sense, even though God used him to deliver true oracles about Israel (Num. 23:2). If God could speak through Balaam's donkey (22:22-30), and communicate His truth to Pharaoh (Gen. 41:15ff), Abimelech (Gen. 20), and Nebuchadnezzar (Dan. 4), then He certainly could speak to and through Balaam. Peter calls Balaam a prophet in 2 Peter 2:15, but the context indicates "false prophet."

3. Since Balaam was in Pethor (22:5), the men had to travel beyond the Euphrates to reach him, a distance of perhaps 350 miles.

4. The fact that Balaam called Jehovah "the Lord my God" (22:18) is no indication that he was a true believer in the God of Israel. Through the Holy Spirit (24:2), God gave Balaam the messages He wanted him to declare, but even this was no proof of saving faith. Balaam spoke the Word of God (22:8; 18, 20, 35, 38; 23:5, 16; 24:4, 16), but he did not have saving faith in the God of the Word. See John 11:45-53 for a parallel.

5. The KJV translates verse 20, "If the men come to call thee," and the ASV (1901) reads, "If the men are come to call thee, rise up, go with them." The Jewish Publication Society translation reads the same way.

6. At least nine times the text tells us that what Balaam spoke was

"the word of the Lord" (22:8, 18, 20, 35, 38; 23:5, 16; 24:4, 16; and see 23:12 and 26). The fact that the man himself was devious and covetous didn't hinder the Spirit (24:2) from using his mind and tongue to communicate inspired truth. In fact, that remarkable experience itself should have brought him to his knees in contrition, but he persisted in his sins.

7. The aim of heathen religion was to control the gods and get them to do what the worshipers wanted, whether it was to defeat their enemies or to give abundant harvests. In bargaining with their gods, the pagan peoples went to all sorts of extremes, even to the point of sacrificing their own children. This kind of "worship" was forbidden in Israel, because Jehovah is totally unlike the pagan gods.

Chapter 10

1. In verse 16, Balaam used three different names for God: El, Elyon (Most High), and Shaddai (Almighty). He had a head knowledge of Israel's God but not a heart relationship with Him.

2. Moses' father-in-law is called both a Kenite (Jud. 1:16) and a Midianite (Num. 10:29).

3. "Numbers" in *The Expositor's Bible Commentary*, Frank E. Gaebelein, General Editor (Grand Rapids: Zondervan, 1990), 913.

4. Some commentators suggest that they did their evil deed right before the tabernacle, or even in the tabernacle precincts, as if to defy the Lord even more. They had done it before Baal over in the Midianite camp, so why not before Jehovah in the camp of Israel? However, the phrase "into the tent" in verse 8 suggests the tent of Zimri and not the tabernacle itself.

5. First Corinthians 10:8 says that 23,000 died, so there seems to be a contradiction. There are several possible answers. Verse 7 suggests that the reference in verse 8 is not to the sin at Baal Peor but at Sinai when the Jews worshiped the golden calf. We aren't told in Exodus 32 how many died because of the golden calf, but Paul tells us in 1 Corinthians 10:8. A second possibility is that only 23,000 died from the plague God sent, but another thousand were slain by the judges (Num. 25:5).

6. F.W. Robertson, *Sermons: Fourth Series* (London: Kegan, Paul,

Trench, Trubner; 1900), 39.

7. The Jerusalem Conference tried to settle this problem (Acts 15:19-29), and Paul dealt with it in 1 Corinthians 8–10. The cheapest meat was sold at the pagan temples, and the guilds (ancient labor unions) often had their meetings and dinners there, so it was tempting to Christians to go along with the crowd.

8. The Greek word translated "sound" gives us the English word "hygiene." Hygeia was the Greek goddess of health.

9. Robertson, 50.

Chapter 11

1. The first census only listed the tribes and the count, but the second census included the clans and families. Since the second census would assist Joshua and Eleazar in assigning each tribe's inheritance, this extra information would be helpful to them.

2. For a study of the Book of Joshua, see my book *Be Strong* (Chariot Victor).

3. This explains why Naboth refused to sell his property to King Ahab (1 Kings 21). See Leviticus 25:23 and Numbers 36:7. Moving or removing a boundary marker was a serious offense in Israel (Deut. 19:14; 27:17; Prov. 22:28; 23:10).

4. The tense of the verb in Deuteronomy. 4:23 indicates that Moses repeatedly begged God to allow him to enter Canaan.

5. In spite of what some hymns and popular Gospel songs say, Canaan is not a picture of heaven. Canaan represents our inheritance now in Jesus Christ as we follow God's Word and claim His promises by faith. God has a special inheritance of life and service for each of His children, and we must trust Him and obey His will. This is one of the major themes of the Book of Hebrews.

6. God instructed Moses to appoint a successor, but there's no record that God gave Joshua the same command before he died. Some "leadership experts" have criticized Joshua for this, but what kind of leader could Joshua appoint without the express commandment of the Lord? Joshua did leave behind a generation of elders who served the Lord, but the next generation turned away from God (Jud. 2:7-11). Moses was the lawgiver who built a great nation out of a collection of slaves, but

Joshua was the general who led that nation in conquering the land and claiming the inheritance. After the conquest of Canaan, the twelve tribes were established in their God-appointed territories, each with its own officers and judges, and the tabernacle and priesthood were in place. The people knew that God was their King, and they had His Law to guide them. The collapse described in the Book of Judges didn't occur because the tribes had no leadership but because the people turned from God their King to the false gods of their neighbors. It was spiritual failure, not organizational or political. The people had failed to obey Deuteronomy 6:1-15.

7. See my book *Be Holy* for an application of these feasts to the Christian life today (Chariot Victor).

8. Firstfruits was celebrated on the day after the Sabbath following Passover, which meant it was always on the first day of the week (Lev. 23:9-14). It speaks to the church today of the resurrection of Jesus Christ on the first day of the week (1 Cor. 15:20-24), the Lord's Day. On that day, the Jewish priest cut a sheaf of grain from the wheat harvest and offered it to God, indicating that the whole harvest belonged to Him. When Christ arose from the dead on that first Lord's Day, He guaranteed our resurrection as well (Rom. 8:18-23; John 12:23-33).

Chapter 12

1. Moab had also been involved in the seduction at Baal Peor (25:1), but since the Moabites were relatives of the Jews, God spared them (Deut. 2:8-9). For the same reason, God wouldn't allow Israel to engage the Ammonites.

2. Once the nation was established, a different law applied to the treatment of captives taken in victories over cities outside the land of Canaan (Deut. 20:1-21:14). However, the conflict with Midian wasn't a normal battle; it was God's punishment of Midian for trying to weaken and destroy His chosen people. He wanted the Midianites to be exterminated so they couldn't pollute the land anymore or tempt His people to sin.

3. That's what Samuel Johnson meant when he said, "Patriotism is the last refuge of a scoundrel." George Bernard Shaw was in agreement when he wrote, "Patriotism is your conviction that this country is supe-

rior to all other countries because you were born in it." A love of country that sees no flaws, pray no prayers, and tries to make no improvements, is idolatry and is dangerous.

4. During the reigns of David and Solomon, the boundaries of the land did approach the borders God set for them. David's conquests reached north to the Euphrates and south to the River of Egypt, and the eastern and western boundaries were expanded.

Titles already available in the
Old Testament
"Be Series"

*Be Amazed (Hosea, Joel, Jonah, Nahum, Habbakuk, Malachi)
*Be Authentic (Genesis 25-50)
 Be Available (Judges)
*Be Basic (Genesis 1-11)
 Be Comforted (Isaiah)
 Be Committed (Ruth, Esther)
*Be Concerned (Amos, Obadiah, Micah, Zephaniah)
 Be Decisive (Jeremiah)
*Be Delivered (Exodus)
 Be Determined (Nehemiah)
*Be Heroic (Haggai, Zechariah, Ezra)
 Be Holy (Leviticus)
 Be Obedient (Life of Abraham/Genesis 12-24)
 Be Patient (Job)
 Be Satisfied (Ecclesiastes)
 Be Skillful (Proverbs)
 Be Strong (Joshua)

*Personal and Group Study Guide Included